COMBUST MOON

PART II

COMBUST MOON

PART II

HIMANSHU SHANGARI

Notion Press Media Pvt Ltd

No. 50, Chettiyar Agaram Main Road,
Vanagaram, Chennai, Tamil Nadu – 600 095

First Published by Notion Press 2022

ISBN
Domestic 978-1-946204-74-5
International 979-8-88883-910-2

Om Namah Shivaay

This book has become possible with the Grace of Lord Shiva and each valuable word in it is due to his blessings.

Om Namah Shivaay

Contents

They Come First

After bowing to Lord Shiva, let me take this moment to bow to the person who has been a strong and supportive influence in my life. She is my respected and adorable mother, **Smt. Jeewan Lata**. So much can be said about her contribution to my life, that a whole book can be written about it. However, I will simply say that even an ocean of words can't describe her true contribution to my life.

After that, I bow to my dear and respected father **Lt. Sh. Bodh Raj Shangari**. Though he left us when I was nine only, the mere fact that he along with my mother brought me to this world, makes me indebted to him for this life as well as for the lives to come. God bless your soul father, wherever you are. Though you are physically not with me, you are always there with me and in me, through all the sweet memories of my childhood, and you will always be.

Prelude

Welcome to the revised edition (2022) of Combust Moon Part 2. Vedic astrology is a very old and comprehensive faith of astrology. Though some other similar faiths are like streams or rivers, Vedic astrology is an ocean which can provide resources to many of these faiths. I have studied and researched many such faiths like Numerology and Vastu, but none of them holds its ground without the support of Vedic astrology. It is the faith which is the backbone of many such faiths.

The fact that Vedic astrology is among the oldest faiths of its kind, also makes it vulnerable to many types of corruptions and adulterations from time to time. Some of these adulterations may be the results of misinterpretations of various concepts of Vedic astrology from time to time. Some others may be there because some scholars may have twisted some definitions, for selfish motives. Due to such adulterations, corruptions and misinterpretations, Vedic astrology may not look as capable and accurate to some people, as it actually is.

With the grace of Lord Shiva, I have spent years in researching various concepts of Vedic astrology. It has been a constant effort to find out where and how much, such concepts may have been misinterpreted; and what could be the correct interpretations of these concepts. Though in their misinterpreted forms, most such concepts of Vedic astrology don't hold ground in real practice of astrology, almost all of them hold solid ground in their modified forms. This effort has taken many years of research, and analysis of thousands of horoscopes. The results, however, have been very rewarding.

This book is an effort to create awareness among the lovers of Vedic astrology that this faith is still as capable as it was when it was born. Various misinterpretations from time to time may have caused confusions related to several important concepts of this faith. Through this series of books, an attempt has been made to create awareness about the concept of Combust Moon.

When a planet comes closer to Sun, more than a safer distance to be maintained, such planet may become weaker as Sun may burn out some of its strength. Such planet that loses some of its strength by virtue of being too close to Sun is called a combust planet. It means when such planet happens to be Moon, it is called combust Moon.

Such combination of Sun and combust Moon can produce a wide variety of results in various houses of horoscope, depending on benefic/malefic nature of these two planets, their signs as well as nakshatras of placements, and on the overall theme of the horoscope under consideration.

This book deals with the placements of Combust Moon in the 4th, 5th and 6th houses of horoscope. Individual chapters have been assigned to Combust Moon in each one of these houses, in different signs. Benefic as well as malefic effects of Combust Moon have been discussed in each one of these houses in different signs, along with relevant examples from horoscopes.

Lord Shiva Bless You

Himanshu Shangari

Combust Moon in Fourth House in Aries

When Sun and combust Moon are placed in the fourth house of a horoscope in Aries, Capricorn rises in the ascendant. Sun rules the eighth house, and Moon rules the seventh house. In general, this combination is partly benefic and partly malefic here, though the malefic part is higher, in most cases. The concept of various planets exhibiting tendencies to be benefic or malefic on the basis of the houses they rule in a horoscope has been explained in the book 'Gemstones: Magic or Science?'.

Combination of Sun and combust Moon in the fourth house of horoscope in Aries is malefic in many cases, though it may turn benefic in some cases. It may happen when such combination is influenced by one or more benefic planets, and/or an overall benefic horoscope. The concept of a malefic planet turning benefic due to influences of benefic planets has been explained in the book 'Match Making and Manglik Dosh'.

When benefic in nature, combination of Sun and combust Moon in the fourth house of a horoscope in Aries can bless the native with good results related to father, mother, marriage, husband, wife, lifespan, education, wealth, properties, vehicles, profession, finances, reputation, authority, recognition, fame and several other good results, depending on his/her overall horoscope and running times.

Such combination of Sun and combust Moon can render various types of benefits to the native, related to or through his father, mother and/or marriage. Considering parents, native's father/mother may be a rich man/woman, a celebrity, an officer in government or a powerful politician. The native may enjoy many benefits because of his father/ mother's money, influence and/or status. He/she may give a big amount of money, and/or wealth to the native, while he/ she's alive, and/or through his/her will. Such combination of Sun and combust Moon can bless the native with good education, vehicles, residential house/houses and/or several other good results. Considering marriage, the native may get married to a woman who may be beautiful, rich, a celebrity, an officer in government, a powerful politician, a successful businesswoman, and/or a citizen of a foreign country. The native may witness several benefits due to or through his wife and/or her family members.

Looking at profession, such combust Moon can help the native achieve success as a fire fighter, fitness trainer, body builder, sportsman, athlete, physician, dietician, lawyer, astrologer, tantric, psychic, spiritual guru, healer, religious guru, teacher, preacher, consultant, actor, singer, musician, writer, dancer, sportsman, artist, architect, designer, developer, poet, chef, interior designer, host, researcher, analyst, professional dealing in education industry, coaching, food, health, pharma, medical, nursing, homecare, real estate, agriculture, hospitality, beauty, fashion, finance, television, music, sports, media, book, publishing, fitness, travel, hotel, airline, fishing, shipping, telecom, computer, software, IT, internet industry or some other type of professional, depending on his/her overall horoscope and running times.

Taking an example, suppose benefic combust Moon is placed in the fourth house of a horoscope in Aries with exalted Sun and retrograde Mercury. Benefic exalted Venus is placed in the third house in Pisces, benefic Saturn is placed in the fifth house in Taurus, benefic Rahu is placed in the seventh house in Cancer with exalted Jupiter; Ketu is placed in the first house in Capricorn, and benefic Mars is placed in the sixth house in Gemini.

In this case, the native may start a company which may deal in various types of trading, including stock trading. He may come across very good amount of success, money and recognition. His business may expand after his age of 35/40, and it may keep growing. If the finer factors and running times are supportive, he may own a business empire worth in billions, by his age of 55/60.

Such combust Moon can bless the native with authority in government as a police officer, army, air force, naval, revenue, administrative, foreign services officer, judge, doctor, scientist, engineer, politician or some other type of professional. Taking an example, suppose benefic combust Moon is placed in the fourth house of a horoscope in Aries with exalted Sun and benefic Mars. Benefic Venus is placed in the sixth house in Gemini with benefic Rahu; Ketu is placed in the twelfth house in Sagittarius, Mercury is placed in the fifth house in Taurus, benefic retrograde Saturn is placed in the eighth house in Leo, and Jupiter is placed in the second house in Aquarius. Ruchaka Yoga and Chandra Mangal Yoga are formed in the fourth house.

In this case, the native may achieve success in civil exams, and he may get selected for the highest possible direct rank in police force. He may serve at several important posts during his career, and he may come across very good amount of success, recognition and authority. If the finer factors and running times are supportive, he may serve at one of the top 2 ranks in police force, before retirement.

On the other hand, when malefic in nature, combination of Sun and combust Moon in the fourth house of a horoscope in Aries can trouble the native with problems related to father, mother, marriage, husband, wife, lifespan, education, wealth, properties, vehicles, profession, finances, reputation, authority, recognition and several other problems, depending on his/her overall horoscope and running times.

Sun rules the eighth house, Moon rules the seventh house, and they are placed in the fourth house. If such combination of Sun and combust Moon is influenced by malefic planets, and/or an overall malefic horoscope, the native may witness various types of problems related to or through his father, mother, marriage and/or lifespan. Considering parents, the native may not have a good equation with his father/mother, his parents may get divorced and he may live with his father/mother, his father/mother may suffer from a long-lasting illness, he/she may be an alcoholic and/or a drug addict, he/she may be a criminal, and/or he/she may die before native's age of 20, depending on native's overall horoscope and running times. He may also witness various types of problems related to properties, vehicles and/or mental health. Considering marriage, the native may witness delay/disturbances in marriage, and/or one or more failed marriages. He may have serious differences of opinion with his wife, she may suffer from a long-lasting illness, she may be an alcoholic and/or a drug addict, she may be a criminal, she may not be loyal to him, she may have extramarital affair/affairs, and/or she may die within 10 or 5 years of marriage. Considering lifespan, the native may witness reduction in lifespan due to several reasons.

The native may witness delays, financial losses, setbacks, failures, job loss, bad reputation and several other problems related to or through his profession. Taking an example, suppose combust Moon is placed in the fourth house of a horoscope in Aries with retrograde Mercury, malefic Rahu and malefic exalted Sun. Malefic Ketu is placed in the tenth house in Libra with Mars; malefic Jupiter is placed in the sixth house in Gemini with Venus; and Saturn is placed in the eighth house in Leo. Grahan Yoga is formed in the fourth house.

In this case, native's mother may die before his age of 10 or 5. His father may get married again, but the native may not have a good equation with his stepmother. His father may die before native's age of 25 or 20. The native may not find a permanent profession till his age of 35/40, or throughout his life. He may remain jobless for periods of more than 3 months, many times in his life. He may witness 1 or 2 failed marriages. He may lose his first wife to death. He may die before his age of 60 or 55, due to some type of Cancer, another fatal disease, or because of a fatal viral infection like COVID.

Combust Moon in Fourth House in Taurus

When Sun and combust Moon are placed in the fourth house of a horoscope in Taurus, Aquarius rises in the ascendant. Sun rules the seventh house, and Moon rules the sixth house. In general, this combination is partly benefic and partly malefic here, though the malefic part is higher, in most cases. The concept of various planets exhibiting tendencies to be benefic or malefic on the basis of the houses they rule in a horoscope has been explained in the book 'Gemstones: Magic or Science?'.

Combination of Sun and combust Moon in the fourth house of horoscope in Taurus is malefic in many cases, though it may turn benefic in some cases. It may happen when such combination is influenced by one or more benefic planets, and/or an overall benefic horoscope. The concept of a malefic planet turning benefic due to influences of benefic planets has been explained in the book 'Match Making and Manglik Dosh'.

When benefic in nature, combination of Sun and combust Moon in the fourth house of a horoscope in Taurus can bless the native with good results related to father, mother, marriage, husband, wife, education, wealth, properties, vehicles, profession, finances, reputation, authority, recognition, fame and several other good results, depending on his/her overall horoscope and running times.

Such combination of Sun and combust Moon can render various types of benefits to the native, related to or through his father, mother and/or marriage. Considering parents, native's father/mother may be a rich man/woman, a celebrity, an officer in government or a powerful politician. The native may enjoy many benefits because of his father/mother's money, influence and/or status. He/she may give a big amount of money, and/or wealth to the native, while he/she's alive, and/or through his/her will. Such combination of Sun and combust Moon can bless the native with good education, vehicles, residential house/houses and/or several other good results. Considering marriage, the native may get married to a woman who may be beautiful, rich, a celebrity, an officer in government, a powerful politician, a successful businesswoman, and/or a citizen of a foreign country. The native may witness several benefits due to or through his wife and/or her family members.

Looking at profession, such combust Moon can help the native achieve success as a fire fighter, fitness trainer, body builder, sportsman, athlete, physician, dietician, lawyer, astrologer, tantric, psychic, spiritual guru, healer, religious guru, teacher, preacher, consultant, actor, singer, musician, writer, dancer, sportsman, artist, architect, designer, developer, poet, chef, interior designer, host, researcher, analyst, professional dealing in education industry, coaching, food, health, pharma, medical, nursing, homecare, real estate, agriculture, hospitality, beauty, fashion, finance, television, music, sports, media, book, publishing, fitness, travel, hotel, airline, fishing, shipping, telecom, computer, software, IT, internet industry or some other type of professional, depending on his/her overall horoscope and running times.

Taking an example, suppose combust Moon is placed in the fourth house of a horoscope in Taurus with benefic Sun and benefic retrograde Venus. Saturn is placed in the eighth house in Virgo with debilitated Ketu; benefic debilitated Rahu is placed in the second house in Pisces, benefic Jupiter is placed in the first house in Aquarius, Mercury is placed in the third house in Aries, and benefic Mars is placed in the ninth house in Libra.

In this case, the native may become an astrologer. He may possess good knowledge of astrology, and he may come across very good amount of success, money and recognition. He may write some books on various topics of astrology. He may also appear on TV programs. If the finer factors and running times are supportive, he may become a very successful astrologer, and his net worth may be in multimillions.

Such combust Moon can bless the native with authority in government as a police officer, army, air force, naval, revenue, administrative, foreign services officer, judge, doctor, scientist, engineer, politician or some other type of professional. Taking an example, suppose combust Moon is placed in the fourth house of a horoscope in Taurus with benefic Sun. Benefic Venus is placed in the third house in Aries with Mercury and debilitated Saturn; benefic Rahu is placed in the first house in Aquarius, benefic Jupiter is placed in the seventh house in Leo with Ketu; and benefic Mars is placed in the eighth house in Virgo.

In this case, the native may achieve success in competitive exams, and he may get selected for the highest possible direct rank in army. He may be a brave officer, and he may succeed in several operations. He may serve at several important posts during his career, and he may come across very good amount of success, recognition and authority. If the finer factors and running times are supportive, he may serve at one of the top 2 ranks in army, before retirement.

On the other hand, when malefic in nature, combination of Sun and combust Moon in the fourth house of a horoscope in Taurus can trouble the native with problems related to father, mother, marriage, husband, wife, education, wealth, properties, vehicles, profession, finances, reputation, authority, recognition and several other problems, depending on his/her overall horoscope and running times.

Sun rules the seventh house, Moon rules the sixth house, and they are placed in the fourth house. If such combination of Sun and combust Moon is influenced by malefic planets, and/or an overall malefic horoscope, the native may witness various types of problems related to or through his father, mother and/or marriage. Considering parents, the native may not have a good equation with his father/mother, his parents may get divorced and he may live with his father/mother, his father/mother may suffer from a long-lasting illness, he/she may be an alcoholic and/or a drug addict, he/she may be a criminal, and/or he/she may die before native's age of 20, depending on native's overall horoscope and running times. He may also witness various types of problems related to properties, vehicles and/or mental health. Considering marriage, the native may witness delay/disturbances in marriage, and/or one or more failed marriages. He may have serious differences of opinion with his wife, she may suffer from a long-lasting illness, she may be an alcoholic and/or a drug addict, she may be a criminal, she may not be loyal to him, she may have extramarital affair/affairs, and/or she may die within 10 or 5 years of marriage.

The native may witness delays, financial losses, setbacks, failures, job loss, bad reputation and several other problems related to or through his profession. Taking an example, suppose malefic combust Moon is placed in the fourth house of a horoscope in Taurus with Sun, Mercury and malefic debilitated Ketu. Malefic debilitated Rahu is placed in the tenth house in Scorpio, retrograde Saturn is placed in the sixth house in Cancer with Venus; Mars is placed in the eighth house in Virgo, and retrograde Jupiter is placed in the twelfth house in Capricorn. Grahan Yoga is formed in the fourth house.

In this case, native's father may die before his age of 10 or 5. His mother may get married again, but the native may not have a good equation with his stepfather. He may not achieve much professional success till his age of 35/40, or throughout his life. He may remain jobless for periods of more than 3 months, many times in his life. He may witness 1 or 2 failed marriages. First marriage of the native may fail due to an extramarital affair that he may have.

Combust Moon in Fourth House in Gemini

When Sun and combust Moon are placed in the fourth house of a horoscope in Gemini, Pisces rises in the ascendant. Sun rules the sixth house, and Moon rules the fifth house. In general, this combination is partly benefic and partly malefic here, though the benefic part is higher, in most cases. The concept of various planets exhibiting tendencies to be benefic or malefic on the basis of the houses they rule in a horoscope has been explained in the book 'Gemstones: Magic or Science?'.

Combination of Sun and combust Moon in the fourth house of horoscope in Gemini is benefic in many cases, though it may turn malefic in some cases. It may happen when such combination is influenced by one or more malefic planets, and/or an overall malefic horoscope. The concept of a benefic planet turning malefic due to influences of malefic planets has been explained in the book 'Match Making and Manglik Dosh'.

When benefic in nature, combination of Sun and combust Moon in the fourth house of a horoscope in Gemini can bless the native with good results related to father, mother, love life, children, creativity, spiritual growth, education, wealth, properties, vehicles, profession, finances, reputation, authority, recognition, fame and several other good results, depending on his/her overall horoscope and running times.

Such combination of Sun and combust Moon can render various types of benefits to the native, related to or through his father, mother and/or children. Considering parents, native's father/mother may be a rich man/woman, a celebrity, an officer in government or a powerful politician. The native may enjoy many benefits because of his father/mother's money, influence and/or status. He/she may give a big amount of money, and/or wealth to the native, while he/she's alive, and/or through his/her will. Such combination of Sun and combust Moon can bless the native with good education, vehicles, residential house/houses and/or several other good results. Considering children, the native may have children who may be physically, intellectually, emotionally, creatively and/or spiritually better or much better than average. Such children may achieve a lot in many spheres of their lives, and they may bring good name and many other good results to the native.

Looking at profession, such combust Moon can help the native achieve success as a fire fighter, fitness trainer, body builder, sportsman, athlete, physician, dietician, lawyer, astrologer, tantric, psychic, spiritual guru, healer, religious guru, teacher, preacher, consultant, researcher, analyst, host, artist, poet, chef, interior designer, professional dealing in education industry, coaching, food, health, pharma, medical, nursing, homecare, real estate, agriculture, hospitality, beauty, fashion, finance, television, music, sports, media, book, publishing, fitness, travel, hotel, airline, fishing, shipping, telecom, computer, software, IT, internet industry or some other type of professional, depending on his/her overall horoscope and running times.

Such combust Moon can help the native achieve success through a creative field as an actor, singer, musician, writer, dancer, sportsman, artist, architect, designer, developer or some other likewise professional. Taking an example, suppose benefic combust Moon is placed in the fourth house of a horoscope in Gemini with Sun and benefic retrograde Mercury. Venus is placed in the third house in Taurus with debilitated Ketu; benefic debilitated Rahu is placed in the ninth house in Scorpio, debilitated Saturn is placed in the second house in Aries, and benefic Jupiter is placed in the seventh house in Virgo with benefic Mars. Mercury forms Bhadra Yoga in the fourth house.

In this case, the native may write fictional books. He may possess remarkable writing talent, and he may come across very good amount of success, money, recognition and fame. He may write in several genres including action, thriller and mystery. He may deliver several bestsellers, and he may receive many awards. If the finer factors and running times are supportive, he may become one of the most successful writers of his time, and his net worth may be in multimillions.

Such combust Moon can bless the native with authority in government as a police officer, army, air force, naval, revenue, administrative, foreign services officer, judge, doctor, scientist, engineer, politician or some other type of professional. Taking an example, suppose benefic combust Moon is placed in the fourth house of a horoscope in Gemini with Sun and benefic Mercury. Benefic Mars is placed in the sixth house in Leo with retrograde Venus; benefic Jupiter forms Hamsa Yoga in the tenth house in Sagittarius, benefic

Rahu is placed in the eighth house in Libra, and Ketu is placed in the second house in Aries with debilitated Saturn. Mercury forms Bhadra Yoga in the fourth house.

In this case, the native may achieve success in civil exams, and he may get selected for the highest possible direct rank in revenue services. He may serve at several important posts during his career, and he may come across very good amount of success, recognition and authority. If the finer factors and running times are supportive, he may serve at one of the top 2 ranks in revenue services, before retirement.

On the other hand, when malefic in nature, combination of Sun and combust Moon in the fourth house of a horoscope in Gemini can trouble the native with problems related to father, mother, love life, children, education, wealth, properties, vehicles, profession, finances, reputation, authority, recognition and several other problems, depending on his/her overall horoscope and running times.

Sun rules the sixth house, Moon rules the fifth house, and they are placed in the fourth house. If such combination of Sun and combust Moon is influenced by malefic planets, and/or an overall malefic horoscope, the native may witness various types of problems related to or through his father, mother and/or children. Considering parents, the native may not have a good equation with his father/mother, his parents may get divorced and he may live with his father/mother, his father/mother may suffer from a long-lasting illness, he/she may be an alcoholic and/or a drug addict, he/she may be a criminal, and/or he/she may die before native's age of 20, depending on native's overall horoscope and running times. He may also witness various types of problems related to properties, vehicles and/or mental health. Considering children, the native may lose one or more children through miscarriages that his wife may witness. He may witness delay in childbirth, and/or he may have children who may be physically and/or mentally troubled in some way. He may lose his children through divorce, or his children may engage in immoral/illegal activities, and he may witness bad reputation and many other problems because of them.

The native may witness delays, financial losses, setbacks, failures, job loss, bad reputation and several other problems related to or through his profession. Taking an example, suppose combust Moon is placed in the fourth house of a horoscope in Gemini with malefic Sun and malefic Venus. Malefic Rahu is placed in the fifth house in Cancer with Mercury; malefic Ketu is placed in the eleventh house in Capricorn with Saturn; Mars is placed in the sixth house in Leo, and Jupiter is placed in the eighth house in Libra.

In this case, native's mother may die before his age of 15 or 10. His father may get married again, but the native may not have a good equation with his stepmother. He may not find a permanent profession throughout his life, and he may only find temporary jobs, though he may earn well at times. He may remain jobless for periods of more than 3 months, many times in his life. He may witness 1 or 2 failed marriages. He may lose one or more children to death, through miscarriages that his wife/wives may witness.

Combust Moon in Fourth House in Cancer

When Sun and combust Moon are placed in the fourth house of a horoscope in Cancer, Aries rises in the ascendant. Sun rules the fifth house, and Moon rules the fourth house. In general, this combination is benefic here, in most cases. The concept of various planets exhibiting tendencies to be benefic or malefic on the basis of the houses they rule in a horoscope has been explained in the book 'Gemstones: Magic or Science?'.

Combination of Sun and combust Moon in the fourth house of horoscope in Cancer is benefic in most cases, though it may turn malefic in some cases. It may happen when such combination is influenced by one or more malefic planets, and/or an overall malefic horoscope. The concept of a benefic planet turning malefic due to influences of malefic planets has been explained in the book 'Match Making and Manglik Dosh'.

When benefic in nature, combination of Sun and combust Moon in the fourth house of a horoscope in Cancer can bless the native with good results related to father, mother, love life, children, creativity, spiritual growth, education, wealth, properties, vehicles, profession, finances, reputation, authority, recognition, fame and several other good results, depending on his/her overall horoscope and running times.

Such combination of Sun and combust Moon can render various types of benefits to the native, related to or through his father, mother and/or children. Considering parents, native's father/mother may be a rich man/woman, a celebrity, an officer in government or a powerful politician. The native may enjoy many benefits because of his father/ mother's money, influence and/or status. He/she may give a big amount of money, and/or wealth to the native, while he/ she's alive, and/or through his/her will. Such combination of Sun and combust Moon can bless the native with good education, vehicles, residential house/houses and/or several other good results. Considering children, the native may have children who may be physically, intellectually, emotionally, creatively and/or spiritually better or much better than average. Such children may achieve a lot in many spheres of their lives, and they may bring good name and many other good results to the native.

Looking at profession, such combust Moon can help the native achieve success as a fire fighter, fitness trainer, body builder, sportsman, athlete, physician, dietician, lawyer, astrologer, tantric, psychic, spiritual guru, healer, religious guru, teacher, preacher, consultant, actor, singer, musician, writer, dancer, sportsman, artist, architect, designer, developer, poet, chef, interior designer, host, researcher, analyst, professional dealing in education industry, coaching, food, health, pharma, medical, nursing, homecare, real estate, agriculture, hospitality, beauty, fashion, finance, television, music, sports, media, book, publishing, fitness, travel, hotel, airline, fishing, shipping, telecom, computer, software, IT, internet industry or some other type of professional, depending on his/her overall horoscope and running times.

Taking an example, suppose benefic combust Moon is placed in the fourth house of a horoscope in Cancer with retrograde Mercury, benefic Sun and benefic Venus. Jupiter is placed in the third house in Gemini with Ketu; benefic Rahu is placed in the ninth house in Sagittarius, and Mars is placed in the sixth house in Virgo. In this case, the native may start a shipping company, and he may witness good results.

If benefic retrograde Saturn is placed in the eleventh house in Aquarius, the equation may become better. In this case, the native may come across very good amount of success, money and recognition through shipping industry. His business may expand after his age of 40/45, and it may keep growing. If the finer factors and running times are supportive, he may own a business empire worth in billions, by his age of 55/60.

Such combust Moon can bless the native with authority in government as a police officer, army, air force, naval, revenue, administrative, foreign services officer, judge, doctor, scientist, engineer, politician or some other type of professional. Taking an example, suppose benefic combust Moon is placed in the fourth house of a horoscope in Cancer with benefic Sun. Benefic Saturn is placed in the third house in Gemini with retrograde Mercury; benefic Venus is placed in the fifth house in Leo with benefic Rahu; and Ketu is placed in the eleventh house in Aquarius with Jupiter. In this case, the native may become an officer in administrative services, and he may enjoy a good career.

If Mars is placed in the ninth house in Sagittarius, the equation may become better. In this case, the native may achieve success in civil exams, and he may get selected for the highest possible direct rank in administrative services. He may serve at several important posts during his career, and he may come across very good amount of success, recognition and authority. If the finer factors and running times are supportive, he may serve as the head of an administrative department, before retirement.

On the other hand, when malefic in nature, combination of Sun and combust Moon in the fourth house of a horoscope in Cancer can trouble the native with problems related to father, mother, love life, children, education, wealth, properties, vehicles, profession, finances, reputation, authority, recognition and several other problems, depending on his/her overall horoscope and running times.

Sun rules the fifth house, Moon rules the fourth house, and they are placed in the fourth house. If such combination of Sun and combust Moon is influenced by malefic planets, and/or an overall malefic horoscope, the native may witness various types of problems related to or through his father, mother and/or children. Considering parents, the native may not have a good equation with his father/mother, his parents may get divorced and he may live with his father/ mother, his father/mother may suffer from a long-lasting illness, he/she may be an alcoholic and/or a drug addict, he/she may be a criminal, and/or he/she may die before native's age of 20, depending on native's overall horoscope and running times. He may also witness various types of problems related to properties, vehicles and/or mental health. Considering children, the native may lose one or more children through miscarriages that his wife may witness. He may witness delay in childbirth, and/or he may have children who may be physically and/or mentally

troubled in some way. He may lose his children through divorce, or his children may engage in immoral/illegal activities, and he may witness bad reputation and many other problems because of them.

The native may witness delays, financial losses, setbacks, failures, job loss, bad reputation and several other problems related to or through his profession. Taking an example, suppose combust Moon is placed in the fourth house of a horoscope in Cancer with Sun, malefic Ketu and malefic retrograde Mercury. Malefic Rahu is placed in the tenth house in Capricorn with debilitated Jupiter; Mars is placed in the fifth house in Leo with benefic Venus; and Saturn is placed in the twelfth house in Pisces. Grahan Yoga is formed in the fourth house whereas Guru Chandal Yoga is formed in the tenth house.

In this case, native's father may die before native's age of 15 or 10. His mother may get married again, but the native may not have a good equation with his stepfather. He may not find a permanent profession till his age of 35/40, or throughout his life, though he may earn well at times. He may witness financial losses and bad reputation through profession. He may witness 2 or 3 failed marriages. He may lose more than one child to death, through miscarriages that his wife/wives may witness.

Combust Moon in Fourth House in Leo

When Sun and combust Moon are placed in the fourth house of a horoscope in Leo, Taurus rises in the ascendant. Sun rules the fourth house, and Moon rules the third house. In general, this combination is benefic here, in most cases. The concept of various planets exhibiting tendencies to be benefic or malefic on the basis of the houses they rule in a horoscope has been explained in the book 'Gemstones: Magic or Science?'.

Combination of Sun and combust Moon in the fourth house of horoscope in Leo is benefic in most cases, though it may turn malefic in some cases. It may happen when such combination is influenced by one or more malefic planets, and/or an overall malefic horoscope. The concept of a benefic planet turning malefic due to influences of malefic planets has been explained in the book 'Match Making and Manglik Dosh'.

When benefic in nature, combination of Sun and combust Moon in the fourth house of a horoscope in Leo can bless the native with good results related to father, mother, siblings, colleagues, education, wealth, properties, vehicles, profession, finances, reputation, authority, recognition, fame and several other good results, depending on his/her overall horoscope and running times.

Such combination of Sun and combust Moon can render various types of benefits to the native, related to or through his father, mother and/or siblings. Considering parents, native's father/mother may be a rich man/woman, a celebrity, an officer in government or a powerful politician.The native may enjoy many benefits because of his father/mother's money, influence and/or status. He/she may give a big amount of money, and/or wealth to the native, while he/she's alive, and/or through his/her will. Such combination of Sun and combust Moon can bless the native with good education, vehicles, residential house/houses and/or several other good results. Considering siblings, some of them may stand by the native and they may help him get out of his problems, many times in his life. A sibling of the native may give him a big amount of money, and/or wealth, while such sibling is alive, and/or through his/her will.

Looking at profession, such combust Moon can help the native achieve success as a fire fighter, fitness trainer, body builder, sportsman, athlete, physician, dietician, lawyer, astrologer, tantric, psychic, spiritual guru, healer, religious guru, teacher, preacher, consultant, actor, singer, musician, writer, dancer, sportsman, artist, architect, designer, developer, poet, chef, interior designer, host, researcher, analyst, professional dealing in education industry, coaching, food, health, pharma, medical, nursing, homecare, real estate, agriculture, hospitality, beauty, fashion, finance, television, music, sports, media, book, publishing, fitness, travel, hotel, airline, fishing, shipping, telecom, computer, software, IT, internet industry or some other type of professional, depending on his/her overall horoscope and running times.

Taking an example, suppose benefic combust Moon is placed in the fourth house of a horoscope in Leo with Venus, retrograde Jupiter and benefic Sun. Benefic Saturn is placed in the second house in Gemini, benefic debilitated Rahu is placed in the eleventh house in Pisces, debilitated Ketu is placed in the fifth house in Virgo, and Mars is placed in the seventh house in Scorpio. In this case, the native may start a company which may deal in real estate projects, and he may witness good results.

If benefic Mercury is placed in the third house in Cancer, the equation may become better. In this case, the native may come across very good amount of success, money and recognition through real estate industry. His business may expand after his age of 35/40, and it may keep growing. His company may deal in big real estate projects including housing societies and commercial complexes. If the finer factors and running times are supportive, he my own a business empire worth in billions, by his age of 55/60.

Such combust Moon can bless the native with authority in government as a police officer, army, air force, naval, revenue, administrative, foreign services officer, judge, doctor, scientist, engineer, politician or some other type of professional. Taking an example, suppose benefic combust Moon is placed in the fourth house of a horoscope in Leo with Venus, benefic Sun and benefic Rahu. Ketu is placed in the tenth house in Aquarius, benefic retrograde Mercury is placed in the third house in Cancer, benefic retrograde Saturn is placed in the eighth house in Sagittarius with Jupiter; and Mars is placed in the first house in Taurus.

In this case, the native may achieve success in civil exams, and he may get selected for the highest possible direct rank in foreign services. He may serve at several important posts during his career, and he may come across very good amount of success, recognition and authority. He may represent his country in several counties of the world. If the finer factors and running times are supportive, he may serve at one of the top 2 ranks in foreign services, before retirement.

On the other hand, when malefic in nature, combination of Sun and combust Moon in the fourth house of a horoscope in Leo can trouble the native with problems related to father, mother, siblings, colleagues, education, wealth, properties, vehicles, profession, finances, reputation, authority, recognition and several other problems, depending on his/her overall horoscope and running times.

Sun rules the fourth house, Moon rules the third house, and they are placed in the fourth house. If such combination of Sun and combust Moon is influenced by malefic planets, and/or an overall malefic horoscope, the native may witness various types of problems related to or through his father, mother and/or siblings. Considering parents, the native may not have a good equation with his father/mother, his parents may get divorced and he may live with his father/mother, his father/mother may suffer from a long-lasting illness, he/she may be an alcoholic and/or a drug addict, he/she may be a criminal, and/or he/she may die before native's age of 20, depending on native's overall horoscope and running times. He may also witness various types of problems related to properties, vehicles and/or mental health. Considering siblings, the native may have bad relationships with some of his siblings, and/or he may witness various types of problems through them or due to them. The native may have siblings who may be criminals, and/or drug addicts, and he may face several problems because of them. In an extreme case, the native may lose one or more siblings to death, before his age of 40 or 35.

The native may witness delays, financial losses, setbacks, failures, job loss, bad reputation and several other problems related to or through his profession. Taking an example, suppose combust Moon is placed in the fourth house of a horoscope in Leo with Sun, malefic Mars and malefic Ketu. Malefic Jupiter is placed in the tenth house in Aquarius with Rahu; benefic exalted Mercury is placed in the fifth house in Virgo, Venus is placed in the sixth house in Libra, and debilitated Saturn is placed in the twelfth house in Aries. Grahan Yoga is formed in the fourth house whereas Guru Chandal Yoga is formed in the tenth house.

In this case, native's father may die before native's age of 15 or 10, and his mother may die before his age of 20 or 15. He may not find a permanent profession till his age of 35/40, or throughout his life, though he may earn well at times. He may witness financial losses, failures and bad reputation through profession. He may lose one or more siblings to death, before his age of 35 or 30. He may witness 1 or 2 failed marriages.

Combust Moon in Fourth House in Virgo

When Sun and combust Moon are placed in the fourth house of a horoscope in Virgo, Gemini rises in the ascendant. Sun rules the third house, and Moon rules the second house. In general, this combination is benefic here, in most cases. The concept of various planets exhibiting tendencies to be benefic or malefic on the basis of the houses they rule in a horoscope has been explained in the book 'Gemstones: Magic or Science?'.

Combination of Sun and combust Moon in the fourth house of horoscope in Virgo is benefic in most cases, though it may turn malefic in some cases. It may happen when such combination is influenced by one or more malefic planets, and/or an overall malefic horoscope. The concept of a benefic planet turning malefic due to influences of malefic planets has been explained in the book 'Match Making and Manglik Dosh'.

When benefic in nature, combination of Sun and combust Moon in the fourth house of a horoscope in Virgo can bless the native with good results related to father, mother, family, speech, siblings, colleagues, education, wealth, properties, vehicles, profession, finances, reputation, authority, recognition, fame and several other good results, depending on his/her overall horoscope and running times.

Such combination of Sun and combust Moon can render various types of benefits to the native, related to or through his father, mother, siblings and/or family. Considering parents, native's father/mother may be a rich man/woman, a celebrity, an officer in government or a powerful politician. The native may enjoy many benefits because of his father/ mother's money, influence and/or status. He/she may give a big amount of money, and/or wealth to the native, while he/ she's alive, and/or through his/her will. Such combination of Sun and combust Moon can bless the native with good education, vehicles, residential house/houses and/or several other good results. Considering siblings, some of them may stand by the native and they may help him get out of his problems, many times in his life. A sibling of the native may give him a big amount of money, and/or wealth, while such sibling is alive, and/or through his/her will.

Looking at profession, such combust Moon can help the native achieve success as a fire fighter, fitness trainer, body builder, sportsman, athlete, physician, dietician, lawyer, astrologer, tantric, psychic, spiritual guru, healer, religious guru, teacher, preacher, consultant, researcher, analyst, host, artist, poet, chef, interior designer, police officer, army, air force, naval, revenue, administrative, foreign services officer, judge, doctor, scientist, engineer, politician, professional dealing in education industry, coaching, food, health, pharma, medical, nursing, homecare, real estate, agriculture, hospitality, beauty, fashion, finance, television, music, sports, media, book, publishing, fitness, travel, hotel, airline, fishing,

shipping, telecom, computer, software, IT, internet industry or some other type of professional, depending on his/her overall horoscope and running times.

Taking an example, suppose benefic combust Moon is placed in the fourth house of a horoscope in Virgo with benefic Sun and benefic exalted Mercury. Venus is placed in the fifth house in Libra, benefic Jupiter is placed in the third house in Leo with Mars; benefic Rahu is placed in the seventh house in Sagittarius, and Saturn is placed in the first house in Gemini with Ketu. Mercury forms Bhadra Yoga in the fourth house whereas Sun and Mercury form Budhaditya Yoga in the same house.

In this case, the native may start a TV channel. He may come across very good amount of success, money and recognition through media industry. His business may expand after his age of 35/40, and it may keep growing. If the finer factors and running times are supportive, he may own a large media network worth in billions, by his age of 55/60.

Such combust Moon can help the native achieve success through a creative field as an actor, singer, musician, writer, dancer, sportsman, artist, architect, designer, developer or some other likewise professional. Taking an example, suppose benefic combust Moon is placed in the fourth house of a horoscope in Virgo with benefic Sun. Benefic Mercury is placed in the fifth house in Libra with Venus and Mars; benefic Rahu is placed in the second house in Cancer, Ketu is placed in the eighth house in Capricorn, and Saturn is placed in the sixth house in Scorpio. In this case, the native may become a singer, and he may witness good results.

If benefic Jupiter is placed in the ninth house in Aquarius, the equation may become better. The native may possess remarkable singing talent, and he may come across very good amount of success, money, recognition and fame. He may deliver several hit songs, and he may receive many awards. He may also write some songs. If the finer factors and running times are supportive, he may become one of the most successful singers of his time, and his net worth may be in multimillions.

On the other hand, when malefic in nature, combination of Sun and combust Moon in the fourth house of a horoscope in Virgo can trouble the native with problems related to father, mother, family, speech, siblings, colleagues, education, wealth, properties, vehicles, profession, finances, reputation, authority, recognition and several other problems, depending on his/her overall horoscope and running times.

Sun rules the third house, Moon rules the second house, and they are placed in the fourth house. If such combination of Sun and combust Moon is influenced by malefic planets, and/or an overall malefic horoscope, the native may witness various types of problems related to or through his father, mother, siblings and/or family. Considering parents, the native may not have a good equation with his father/mother, his parents may get divorced and he may live with his father/mother, his father/mother may suffer from a long-lasting illness, he/she may be an alcoholic and/or a drug addict, he/she may be a criminal, and/or he/she may die before native's age of 20, depending on native's overall horoscope and running times. He may also witness various types of problems related to properties, vehicles and/or mental health. Considering siblings, the native may have bad relationships with some of his siblings, and/or he may witness various types of problems through them or due to them. The native may have siblings who may be criminals, and/or drug addicts, and he may face several problems because of them. In an extreme case, the native may lose one or more siblings to death, before his age of 40 or 35.

The native may witness delays, financial losses, setbacks, failures, job loss, bad reputation and several other problems related to or through his profession. Taking an example, suppose combust Moon is placed in the fourth house of a horoscope in Virgo with Sun, retrograde Saturn and malefic exalted Rahu. Malefic exalted Ketu is placed in the tenth house in Pisces, benefic retrograde Mercury is placed in the third house in Leo, malefic Mars is placed in the fifth house in Libra with Venus; and Jupiter is placed in the sixth house in Scorpio. Grahan Yoga is formed in the fourth house.

In this case, native's father may die before native's age of 15 or 10. His mother may get married again, but the native may not have a good equation with his stepfather. The native may not find a permanent profession throughout his life, and he may keep losing jobs, though he may earn well at times. He may remain jobless for periods of more than 3 months, many times in his life. He may witness several problems because of some of his siblings, including financial losses and betrayals. He may witness 2 or 3 failed marriages.

Combust Moon in Fourth House in Libra

When Sun and combust Moon are placed in the fourth house of a horoscope in Libra, Cancer rises in the ascendant. Sun rules the second house, and Moon rules the first house. In general, this combination is benefic here, in most cases. The concept of various planets exhibiting tendencies to be benefic or malefic on the basis of the houses they rule in a horoscope has been explained in the book 'Gemstones: Magic or Science?'.

Combination of Sun and combust Moon in the fourth house of horoscope in Libra is benefic in most cases, though it may turn malefic in some cases. It may happen when such combination is influenced by one or more malefic planets, and/or an overall malefic horoscope. The concept of a benefic planet turning malefic due to influences of malefic planets has been explained in the book 'Match Making and Manglik Dosh'.

When benefic in nature, combination of Sun and combust Moon in the fourth house of a horoscope in Libra can bless the native with good results related to father, mother, health, lifespan, family, speech, education, wealth, properties, vehicles, profession, finances, reputation, authority, recognition, fame and several other good results, depending on his/her overall horoscope and running times.

Such combination of Sun and combust Moon can render various types of benefits to the native, related to or through his father, mother, family and/or lifespan. Considering parents, native's father/mother may be a rich man/woman, a celebrity, an officer in government or a powerful politician. The native may enjoy many benefits because of his father/mother's money, influence and/or status. He/she may give a big amount of money, and/or wealth to the native, while he/she's alive, and/or through his/her will. Such combination of Sun and combust Moon can bless the native with good education, vehicles, residential house/houses and/or several other good results. Considering family, the native may be born in a rich, influential, resourceful, well-respected, politically powerful, royal and/or spiritually advanced family, and he may witness several benefits by virtue of being a member of such family. The native may be a good, very good or gifted speaker, and he may achieve good results in many spheres of his life, by virtue of his speech abilities.

Looking at profession, such combust Moon can help the native achieve success as a fire fighter, fitness trainer, body builder, sportsman, athlete, physician, dietician, lawyer, astrologer, tantric, psychic, spiritual guru, healer, religious guru, teacher, preacher, consultant, researcher, analyst, host, artist, poet, chef, interior designer, police officer, army, air force, naval, revenue, administrative, foreign services officer, judge, doctor, scientist, engineer, politician, professional dealing in education industry, coaching, food, health, pharma, medical, nursing, homecare, real estate, agriculture, hospitality, beauty, fashion, finance, television, music, sports, media, book, publishing, fitness, travel, hotel, airline, fishing, shipping, telecom, computer, software, IT, internet industry or some other type of professional, depending on his/her overall horoscope and running times.

Taking an example, suppose benefic combust Moon is placed in the fourth house of a horoscope in Libra with benefic Venus and benefic debilitated Sun. Exalted Mercury is placed in the third house in Virgo, benefic exalted Rahu is placed in the eleventh house in Taurus with Jupiter; exalted Ketu is placed in the fifth house in Scorpio, benefic Mars is placed in the second house in Leo, and Saturn is placed in the seventh house in Capricorn. Venus forms Malavya Yoga whereas Sun and Venus form Neechbhang Rajyoga in the fourth house.

In this case, the native may start a hotel, and he may come across very good amount of success, money and recognition. His business may expand after his age of 35/40, and it may keep growing. If the finer factors and running times are supportive, he may own several hotels worth in billions, by his age of 55/60.

Such combust Moon can help the native achieve success through a creative field as an actor, singer, musician, writer, dancer, sportsman, artist, architect, designer, developer or some other likewise professional. Taking an example for a female native, suppose benefic combust Moon is placed in the fourth house of a horoscope in Libra with Mercury, benefic Venus and benefic debilitated Sun. Benefic Rahu is placed in the second house in Leo with Jupiter and Saturn; Ketu is placed in the eighth house in Aquarius, and benefic debilitated Mars is placed in the first house in Cancer. Malavya Yoga and Neechbhang Rajyoga are formed in the fourth house.

In this case, the native may become an actor, and she may come across very good amount of success, money, recognition and fame. She may perform well in the genres of drama, romance and comedy. She may deliver several hit movies, and she may receive awards. If the finer factors and running times are supportive, she may become a successful actor, and her net worth may be in multimillions.

On the other hand, when malefic in nature, combination of Sun and combust Moon in the fourth house of a horoscope in Libra can trouble the native with problems related to father, mother, health, lifespan, family, speech, education, wealth, properties, vehicles, profession, finances, reputation, authority, recognition and several other problems, depending on his/her overall horoscope and running times.

Sun rules the second house, Moon rules the first house, and they are placed in the fourth house. If such combination of Sun and combust Moon is influenced by malefic planets, and/or an overall malefic horoscope, the native may witness various types of problems related to or through his father, mother, family and/or lifespan. Considering parents, the native may not have a good equation with his father/mother, his parents may get divorced and he may live with his father/ mother, his father/mother may suffer from a long-lasting illness, he/she may be an alcoholic and/or a drug addict, he/she may be a criminal, and/or he/she may die before native's age of 20, depending on native's overall horoscope and running times. He may also witness various types of problems related to properties, vehicles and/or mental health. Considering family, the native may be born in a family which may be poor, and/or some of his family members may be alcoholics, drug addicts, criminals and/or they may have some other negative traits. Hence the native may witness several problems in his life, due to bad reputation of his family, and/or bad conducts of some family members. Considering lifespan, the native may witness reduction in lifespan due to several reasons.

The native may witness delays, financial losses, setbacks, failures, job loss, bad reputation and several other problems related to or through his profession. Taking an example, suppose combust Moon is placed in the fourth house of a horoscope in Libra with debilitated Sun, malefic Mercury and malefic exalted Saturn. Malefic Rahu is placed in the sixth house in Sagittarius with Venus; malefic Ketu is placed in the twelfth house in Gemini with Jupiter; and Mars is placed in the eighth house in Aquarius. Guru Chandal Yoga is formed in the twelfth house.

In this case, native's father may die before native's age of 15 or 10. The native may not have a good equation with his mother. He may not find a permanent profession throughout his life, and he may only find temporary jobs. He may remain jobless for periods of more than 3 months, many times in his life. He may lose one or more siblings to death, before his age of 40/35. He may witness 1 or 2 failed marriages. He may die before his age of 60 or 55, due to a heart attack, some type of cancer, in an accident, or because of a fatal viral infection like COVID.

Combust Moon in Fourth House in Scorpio

When Sun and combust Moon are placed in the fourth house of a horoscope in Scorpio, Leo rises in the ascendant. Sun rules the first house, and Moon rules the twelfth house. In general, this combination is partly benefic and partly malefic here, though the benefic part is higher, in most cases. The concept of various planets exhibiting tendencies to be benefic or malefic on the basis of the houses they rule in a horoscope has been explained in the book 'Gemstones: Magic or Science?'.

Combination of Sun and combust Moon in the fourth house of horoscope in Scorpio is benefic in many cases, though it may turn malefic in some cases. It may happen when such combination is influenced by one or more malefic planets, and/or an overall malefic horoscope. The concept of a benefic planet turning malefic due to influences of malefic planets has been explained in the book 'Match Making and Manglik Dosh'.

When benefic in nature, combination of Sun and combust Moon in the fourth house of a horoscope in Scorpio can bless the native with good results related to father, mother, health, lifespan, creativity, spiritual growth, education, wealth, properties, vehicles, profession, finances, reputation, authority, recognition, fame and several other good results, depending on his/her overall horoscope and running times.

Such combination of Sun and combust Moon can render various types of benefits to the native, related to or through his father, mother and/or lifespan. Considering parents, native's father/mother may be a rich man/woman, a celebrity, an officer in government or a powerful politician. The native may enjoy many benefits because of his father/ mother's money, influence and/or status. He/she may give a big amount of money, and/or wealth to the native, while he/ she's alive, and/or through his/her will. Such combination of Sun and combust Moon can bless the native with good education, vehicles, residential house/houses and/or several other good results.

Looking at profession, such combust Moon can help the native achieve success as a fire fighter, fitness trainer, body builder, sportsman, athlete, physician, dietician, lawyer, astrologer, tantric, psychic, spiritual guru, healer, religious guru, teacher, preacher, consultant, researcher, analyst, host, artist, poet, chef, interior designer, professional dealing in education industry, coaching, food, health, pharma, medical, nursing, homecare, real estate, agriculture, hospitality, beauty, fashion, finance, television, music, sports, media, book, publishing, fitness, travel, hotel, airline, fishing, shipping, telecom, computer, software, IT, internet industry or some other type of professional, depending on his/her overall horoscope and running times.

Such combust Moon can help the native achieve success through a creative field as an actor, singer, musician, writer,

dancer, sportsman, artist, architect, designer, developer or some other likewise professional. Taking an example, suppose combust Moon is placed in the fourth house of a horoscope in Scorpio with benefic Sun. Benefic Mercury is placed in the third house in Libra, benefic Mars is placed in the eleventh house in Gemini, benefic Rahu is placed in the twelfth house in Cancer with Saturn; Ketu is placed in the sixth house in Capricorn, and Jupiter is placed in the second house in Virgo. In this case, the native may write fictional books, and he may witness good results.

If benefic Venus is placed in the third house in Libra with Mercury; the equation may become better. The native may possess remarkable writing talent, and he may come across very good amount of success, money, recognition and fame. He may write in several genres including mystery, fantasy and science-fiction. He may deliver several bestsellers, and he may receive many awards. If the finer factors and running times are supportive, he may become one of the most successful writers of his time, and his net worth may be in multimillions.

Such combust Moon can bless the native with authority in government as a police officer, army, air force, naval, revenue, administrative, foreign services officer, judge, doctor, scientist, engineer, politician or some other type of professional. Taking an example, suppose combust Moon is placed in the fourth house of a horoscope in Scorpio with benefic Sun, benefic Venus and benefic retrograde Mercury. Benefic Mars is placed in the first house in Leo with benefic Rahu; Ketu is placed in the seventh house in Aquarius, and retrograde Jupiter is placed in the ninth house in Aries with retrograde Saturn. Sun and Mercury form Budhaditya Yoga in the fourth house.

In this case, the native may join air force of his country. He may achieve success in competitive exams, and he may get selected for the highest possible direct rank in air force. He may be a skilled fighter pilot, and he may succeed in several missions. He may serve at several important posts during his career, and he may come across very good amount of success, recognition and authority. If the finer factors and running times are supportive, he may serve as the chief of air force of his country, before retirement.

On the other hand, when malefic in nature, combination of Sun and combust Moon in the fourth house of a horoscope in Scorpio can trouble the native with problems related to father, mother, health, lifespan, education, wealth, properties, vehicles, profession, finances, reputation, authority, recognition and several other problems, depending on his/her overall horoscope and running times.

Sun rules the first house, Moon rules the twelfth house, and they are placed in the fourth house. If such combination of Sun and combust Moon is influenced by malefic planets, and/or an overall malefic horoscope, the native may witness various types of problems related to or through his father, mother and/or lifespan. Considering parents, the native may not have a good equation with his father/mother, his parents may get divorced and he may live with his father/mother, his father/mother may suffer from a long-lasting illness, he/she may be an alcoholic and/or a drug addict, he/she may be a criminal, and/or he/she may die before native's age of 20, depending on native's overall horoscope and running times. He may also witness various types of problems related to properties, vehicles and/or mental health. Considering lifespan, the native may witness reduction in lifespan due to several reasons. For example, the native may die in an accident, through a natural disaster, due to a fatal disease, due to a fatal viral infection like COVID, due to drug addiction, he may commit suicide, or someone may kill him intentionally or unintentionally. Considering some unintentional incidents, he may get caught in a crossfire between two rival criminal gangs or that between criminals and police, or someone may accidently kill him.

The native may witness delays, financial losses, setbacks, failures, job loss, bad reputation and several other problems related to or through his profession. Taking an example, suppose malefic combust Moon is placed in the fourth house of a horoscope in Scorpio with Sun, retrograde Mercury, malefic retrograde Saturn and malefic exalted Ketu. Malefic exalted Rahu is placed in the tenth house in Taurus, Venus is placed in the sixth house in Capricorn with debilitated Jupiter; and Mars is placed in the eighth house in Pisces. Grahan Yoga is formed in the fourth house.

In this case, native's father as well as mother may die before his age of 15 or 10. He may not achieve much professional success till his age of 35/40, or throughout his life. He may witness financial tightness, debts and bad reputation, many times in his life. He may witness 1 or 2 failed marriages. He may die before his age of 60 or 55, due to a fatal disease, or because of a fatal viral infection like COVID or HIV AIDS.

Combust Moon in Fourth House in Sagittarius

When Sun and combust Moon are placed in the fourth house of a horoscope in Sagittarius, Virgo rises in the ascendant. Sun rules the twelfth house, and Moon rules the eleventh house. In general, this combination is partly benefic and partly malefic here, though the malefic part is higher, in most cases. The concept of various planets exhibiting tendencies to be benefic or malefic on the basis of the houses they rule in a horoscope has been explained in the book 'Gemstones: Magic or Science?'.

Combination of Sun and combust Moon in the fourth house of horoscope in Sagittarius is malefic in many cases, though it may turn benefic in some cases. It may happen when such combination is influenced by one or more benefic planets, and/or an overall benefic horoscope. The concept of a malefic planet turning benefic due to influences of benefic planets has been explained in the book 'Match Making and Manglik Dosh'.

When benefic in nature, combination of Sun and combust Moon in the fourth house of a horoscope in

Sagittarius can bless the native with good results related to father, mother, creativity, spiritual growth, friends, education, wealth, properties, vehicles, profession, finances, reputation, authority, recognition, fame and several other good results, depending on his/her overall horoscope and running times.

Such combination of Sun and combust Moon can render various types of benefits to the native, related to or through his father, mother and/or friends. Considering parents, native's father/mother may be a rich man/woman, a celebrity, an officer in government or a powerful politician. The native may enjoy many benefits because of his father/mother's money, influence and/or status. He/she may give a big amount of money, and/or wealth to the native, while he/she's alive, and/or through his/her will. Such combination of Sun and combust Moon can bless the native with good education, vehicles, residential house/houses and/or several other good results. Considering friends, some of his friends may stand by the native and they may help him get out of his problems, many times in his life. One or more of his friends may help him financially as well as in other ways, in order for him to start a new business, or repair/consolidate an already existing business.

Looking at profession, such combust Moon can help the native achieve success as a fire fighter, fitness trainer, body builder, sportsman, athlete, physician, dietician, lawyer, astrologer, tantric, psychic, spiritual guru, healer, religious guru, teacher, preacher, consultant, researcher, analyst, host, artist, poet, chef, interior designer, police officer, army, air force, naval, revenue, administrative, foreign services officer, judge, doctor, scientist, engineer, politician, professional dealing in education industry, coaching, food, health, pharma, medical, nursing, homecare, real estate, agriculture, hospitality, beauty, fashion, finance, television, music, sports, media, book, publishing, fitness, travel, hotel, airline, fishing, shipping, telecom, computer, software, IT, internet industry or some other type of professional, depending on his/her overall horoscope and running times.

Taking an example, suppose benefic combust Moon is placed in the fourth house of a horoscope in Sagittarius with Sun, benefic Mercury and benefic Venus. Benefic retrograde Jupiter is placed in the eleventh house in Cancer with benefic Rahu; Ketu is placed in the fifth house in Capricorn, Saturn is placed in the seventh house in Pisces, and Mars is placed in the ninth house in Taurus.

In this case, the native may start an airline, and he may come across very good amount of success, money and recognition. His business may expand after his age of 40/45, and it may keep growing. He may also invest in hotel and/or real estate industry, and he may witness profits. If the finer factors and running times are supportive, he may own a business empire worth in billions, by his age of 55/60.

Such combust Moon can help the native achieve success through a creative field as an actor, singer, musician, writer, dancer, sportsman, artist, architect, designer, developer or some other likewise professional. Taking an example, suppose benefic combust Moon is placed in the fourth house of a horoscope in Sagittarius with Sun and benefic Mercury. Benefic Venus is placed in the fifth house in Capricorn with Saturn; benefic exalted Rahu is placed in the ninth house in Taurus, exalted Ketu is placed in the third house in Scorpio, and Mars is placed in the second house in Libra. In this case, the native may become a movie director, and he may witness good results.

If benefic Jupiter is placed in the ninth house in Taurus with Rahu; the equation may become better. The native may possess remarkable talent as a director, and he may come across very good amount of success, money, recognition and fame. He may deliver several hit movies, and he may receive many awards. If the finer factors and running times are supportive, he may become one of the most successful directors of his time, and his net worth may be in multimillions.

On the other hand, when malefic in nature, combination of Sun and combust Moon in the fourth house of a horoscope in Sagittarius can trouble the native with problems related to father, mother, friends, education, wealth, properties, vehicles, profession, finances, reputation, authority, recognition and several other problems, depending on his/her overall horoscope and running times.

Sun rules the twelfth house, Moon rules the eleventh house, and they are placed in the fourth house. If such combination of Sun and combust Moon is influenced by malefic planets, and/or an overall malefic horoscope, the native may witness various types of problems related to or through his father, mother and/or friends. Considering parents, the native may not have a good equation with his father/mother, his parents may get divorced and he may live with his father/mother, his father/mother may suffer from a long-lasting illness, he/she may be an alcoholic and/or a drug addict, he/she may be a criminal, and/or he/she may die before native's age of 20, depending on native's overall horoscope and running times. He may also witness various types of problems related to properties, vehicles and/or mental health. Considering friends, some of his friends may be selfish, opportunists, criminal-minded, criminals, drug addicts, traitors and/or they may have some other negative traits. The native may witness several problems because of such friends, many times in his life. Some of his friends may be his hidden enemies, and they may keep causing problems for him. In an extreme case, one or more of his good friends may die before native's age of 40 or 35.

The native may witness delays, financial losses, setbacks, failures, job loss, bad reputation and several other problems related to or through his profession. Taking an example, suppose combust Moon is placed in the fourth house of a horoscope in Sagittarius with malefic Sun and malefic Rahu. Malefic Ketu is placed in the tenth house in Gemini, Mercury is placed in the fifth house in Capricorn, Venus is placed in the sixth house in Aquarius with Jupiter; and malefic Mars is placed in the ninth house in Taurus with retrograde Saturn. Grahan Yoga is formed in the fourth house.

In this case, native's father may die before native's age of 10 or 5. His mother may get married again, but the native may not have a good equation with his stepfather. The native may not find a permanent profession till his age of 35/40, or throughout his life, though he may earn well at times. He may remain jobless for periods of more than 3 months, many times in his life. He may face several problems because of some of his friends, including financial losses and bad reputation. He may witness 1 or 2 failed marriages.

Combust Moon in Fourth House in Capricorn

When Sun and combust Moon are placed in the fourth house of a horoscope in Capricorn, Libra rises in the ascendant. Sun rules the eleventh house, and Moon rules the tenth house. In general, this combination is benefic here, in most cases. The concept of various planets exhibiting tendencies to be benefic or malefic on the basis of the houses they rule in a horoscope has been explained in the book 'Gemstones: Magic or Science?'.

Combination of Sun and combust Moon in the fourth house of horoscope in Capricorn is benefic in most cases, though it may turn malefic in some cases. It may happen when such combination is influenced by one or more malefic planets, and/or an overall malefic horoscope. The concept of a benefic planet turning malefic due to influences of malefic planets has been explained in the book 'Match Making and Manglik Dosh'.

When benefic in nature, combination of Sun and combust Moon in the fourth house of a horoscope in Capricorn can bless the native with good results related to father, mother, friends, education, wealth, properties, vehicles, profession, finances, reputation, authority, recognition, fame and several other good results, depending on his/her overall horoscope and running times.

Such combination of Sun and combust Moon can render various types of benefits to the native, related to or through his father, mother and/or friends. Considering parents, native's father/mother may be a rich man/woman, a celebrity, an officer in government or a powerful politician. The native may enjoy many benefits because of his father/mother's money, influence and/or status. He/she may give a big amount of money, and/or wealth to the native, while he/she's alive, and/or through his/her will. Such combination of Sun and combust Moon can bless the native with good education, vehicles, residential house/houses and/or several other good results. Considering friends, some of his friends may stand by the native and they may help him get out of his problems, many times in his life. One or more of his friends may help him financially as well as in other ways, in order for him to start a new business, or repair/consolidate an already existing business.

Looking at profession, such combust Moon can help the native achieve success as a fire fighter, fitness trainer, body builder, sportsman, athlete, physician, dietician, lawyer, astrologer, tantric, psychic, spiritual guru, healer, religious guru, teacher, preacher, consultant, researcher, analyst, host, artist, poet, chef, interior designer, professional dealing in education industry, coaching, food, health, pharma, medical, nursing, homecare, real estate, agriculture, hospitality, beauty, fashion, finance, television, music, sports, media, book, publishing, fitness, travel, hotel, airline, fishing, shipping, telecom, computer, software, IT, internet industry or some other type of professional, depending on his/her overall horoscope and running times.

Such combust Moon can help the native achieve success through a creative field as an actor, singer, musician, writer, dancer, sportsman, artist, architect, designer, developer or some other likewise professional. Taking an example, suppose benefic combust Moon is placed in the fourth house of a horoscope in Capricorn with retrograde Jupiter and benefic Sun. Benefic Saturn is placed in the sixth house in Pisces with exalted Venus; Mercury is placed in the fifth house in Aquarius, benefic debilitated Rahu is placed in the second house in Scorpio, and debilitated Ketu is placed in the eighth house in Taurus. In this case, the native may become a fashion designer, and he may witness good results.

If benefic Mars is placed in the third house in Sagittarius, the equation may become better. The native may start a company which may make various types of fashion products, and he may come across very good amount of success, money and recognition, along with good amount of fame. His business may expand after his age of 35/40, and it may keep growing. If the finer factors and running times are supportive, he may become one of the most successful fashion designers of his time, and he may own a business empire worth in billions, by his age of 55/60.

Such combust Moon can bless the native with authority in government as a police officer, army, air force, naval, revenue, administrative, foreign services officer, judge, doctor, scientist, engineer, politician or some other type of professional. Taking an example, suppose benefic combust Moon is placed in the fourth house of a horoscope in Capricorn with Venus and benefic Sun. Benefic exalted Saturn forms Shasha Yoga in the first house in Libra, Mercury is placed in the third house in

Sagittarius with retrograde Jupiter; benefic Mars is placed in the sixth house in Pisces with benefic debilitated Rahu; and debilitated Ketu is placed in the twelfth house in Virgo.

In this case, the native may engage in politics, and he may come across very good amount of success, recognition, authority and fame. He may win several elections, and he may become a minister in national government, more than once. He may hold ministry of home, health, law, finance and/ or defence affairs. If the finer factors and running times are supportive, he may serve as prime minister or president of his country.

On the other hand, when malefic in nature, combination of Sun and combust Moon in the fourth house of a horoscope in Capricorn can trouble the native with problems related to father, mother, friends, education, wealth, properties, vehicles, profession, finances, reputation, authority, recognition and several other problems, depending on his/ her overall horoscope and running times.

Sun rules the eleventh house, Moon rules the tenth house, and they are placed in the fourth house. If such combination of Sun and combust Moon is influenced by malefic planets, and/or an overall malefic horoscope, the native may witness various types of problems related to or through his father, mother and/or friends. Considering parents, the native may not have a good equation with his father/mother, his parents may get divorced and he may live with his father/mother, his father/mother may suffer from a long-lasting illness, he/ she may be an alcoholic and/or a drug addict, he/she may be a criminal, and/or he/she may die before native's age of 20, depending on native's overall horoscope and running times. He may also witness various types of problems related to properties, vehicles and/or mental health. Considering friends, some of his friends may be selfish, opportunists, criminal-minded, criminals, drug addicts, traitors and/or they may have some other negative traits. The native may witness several problems because of such friends, many times in his life. Some of his friends may be his hidden enemies, and they may keep causing problems for him. In an extreme case, one or more of his good friends may die before native's age of 40 or 35.

The native may witness delays, financial losses, setbacks, failures, job loss, bad reputation and several other problems related to or through his profession. Taking an example, suppose combust Moon is placed in the fourth house of a horoscope in Capricorn with Sun, Mercury, malefic Ketu and malefic retrograde Jupiter. Malefic Rahu is placed in the tenth house in Cancer, exalted Venus is placed in the sixth house in Pisces with Saturn; and Mars is placed in the twelfth house in Virgo. Grahan Yoga as well as Guru Chandal Yoga is formed in the fourth house.

In this case, native's father as well as mother may die before his age of 20 or 15. He may not achieve much professional success till his age of 35/40, or throughout his life, though he may earn well at times. He may remain jobless for periods of more than 3 months, many times in his life. He may lose one or more good friends to death, before his age of 35/30. He may not get married till his age of 35/40, or throughout his life.

Combust Moon in Fourth House in Aquarius

When Sun and combust Moon are placed in the fourth house of a horoscope in Aquarius, Scorpio rises in the ascendant. Sun rules the tenth house, and Moon rules the ninth house. In general, this combination is benefic here, in most cases. The concept of various planets exhibiting tendencies to be benefic or malefic on the basis of the houses they rule in a horoscope has been explained in the book 'Gemstones: Magic or Science?'.

Combination of Sun and combust Moon in the fourth house of horoscope in Aquarius is benefic in most cases, though it may turn malefic in some cases. It may happen when such combination is influenced by one or more malefic planets, and/or an overall malefic horoscope. The concept of a benefic planet turning malefic due to influences of malefic planets has been explained in the book 'Match Making and Manglik Dosh'.

When benefic in nature, combination of Sun and combust Moon in the fourth house of a horoscope in Aquarius can bless the native with good results related to father, mother, creativity, spiritual growth, education, wealth, properties, vehicles, profession, finances, reputation, authority, recognition, fame and several other good results, depending on his/her overall horoscope and running times.

Such combination of Sun and combust Moon can render various types of benefits to the native, related to or through his father and/or mother. Considering parents, native's father/mother may be a rich man/woman, a celebrity, an officer in government or a powerful politician. The native may enjoy many benefits because of his father/mother's money, influence and/or status. He/she may give a big amount of money, and/or wealth to the native, while he/she's alive, and/or through his/her will. Such combination of Sun and combust Moon can bless the native with good education, vehicles, residential house/houses and/or several other good results.

Looking at profession, such combust Moon can help the native achieve success as a fire fighter, fitness trainer, body builder, sportsman, athlete, physician, dietician, lawyer, astrologer, tantric, psychic, spiritual guru, healer, religious guru, teacher, preacher, consultant, researcher, analyst, host, artist, poet, chef, interior designer, professional dealing in education industry, coaching, food, health, pharma, medical, nursing, homecare, real estate, agriculture, hospitality, beauty, fashion, finance, television, music, sports, media, book, publishing, fitness, travel, hotel, airline, fishing, shipping, telecom, computer, software, IT, internet industry or some other type of professional, depending on his/her overall horoscope and running times.

Such combust Moon can help the native achieve success through a creative field as an actor, singer, musician, writer, dancer, sportsman, artist, architect, designer, developer or some other likewise professional. Taking an example, suppose benefic combust Moon is placed in the fourth house of a horoscope in Aquarius with Venus and benefic Sun. Retrograde Mercury is placed in the fifth house in Pisces with exalted Ketu; benefic exalted Rahu is placed in the eleventh house in Virgo, Mars is placed in the eighth house in Gemini, and benefic Saturn is placed in the ninth house in Cancer. In this case, the native may write fictional books, and he may witness good results.

If benefic retrograde Jupiter is placed in the ninth house in Cancer with Saturn; the equation may become better. The native may possess remarkable writing talent, and he may come across very good amount of success, money, recognition and fame. He may write in several genres including mystery, thriller and paranormal. He may deliver several bestsellers, and he may receive many awards. If the finer factors and running times are supportive, he may become one of the most successful writers of his time, and his net worth may be in multimillions.

Such combust Moon can bless the native with authority in government as a police officer, army, air force, naval, revenue, administrative, foreign services officer, judge, doctor, scientist, engineer, politician or some other type of professional. Taking an example, suppose benefic combust Moon is placed in the fourth house of a horoscope in Aquarius with retrograde Mercury and benefic Sun. Venus is placed in the sixth house in Aries, debilitated Mars is placed in the ninth house in Cancer, benefic Rahu is placed in the eighth house in Gemini, Ketu is placed in the second house in Sagittarius, and benefic Jupiter is placed in the seventh house in Taurus. In this case, the native may become an officer in administrative services, and he may enjoy a good career.

If benefic Saturn is placed in the fourth house in Aquarius with Sun, Moon and Mercury; the equation may become better. Saturn forms Shasha Yoga in the fourth house. In this case, the native may achieve success in civil exams, and he may get selected for the highest possible direct rank in administrative services. He may serve at several important posts during his career, and he may come across very good amount of success, recognition and authority. If the finer factors and running times are supportive, he may serve as the head of an administrative department, before retirement.

On the other hand, when malefic in nature, combination of Sun and combust Moon in the fourth house of a horoscope in Aquarius can trouble the native with problems related to father, mother, education, wealth, properties, vehicles, profession, finances, reputation, authority, recognition and several other problems, depending on his/her overall horoscope and running times.

Sun rules the tenth house; Moon rules the ninth house, and they are placed in the fourth house. If such combination of Sun and combust Moon is influenced by malefic planets, and/or an overall malefic horoscope, the native may witness various types of problems related to or through his father and/or mother. Considering parents, the native may not have a good equation with his father/mother, his parents may get divorced and he may live with his father/mother, his father/mother may suffer from a long-lasting illness, he/she may be an alcoholic and/or a drug addict, he/she may be a criminal, and/or he/she may die before native's age of 20, depending on native's overall horoscope and running times. He may also witness various types of problems related to properties, vehicles and/or mental health.

The native may witness delays, financial losses, setbacks, failures, job loss, bad reputation and several other problems related to or through his profession. Taking an example, suppose combust Moon is placed in the fourth house of a horoscope in Aquarius with Sun, malefic Mercury and malefic Venus. Malefic Rahu is placed in the twelfth house in Libra, malefic Ketu is placed in the sixth house in Aries with debilitated Saturn; Jupiter is placed in the eighth house in Gemini, and Mars is placed in the seventh house in Taurus.

In this case, native's father as well as mother may die before his age of 15 or 10. He may not find a permanent profession throughout his life, and he may only find temporary jobs. He may witness financial losses and bad reputation through profession. He may remain jobless for periods of more than 3 months, many times in his life. He may witness 1 or 2 failed marriages.

Combust Moon in Fourth House in Pisces

When Sun and combust Moon are placed in the fourth house of a horoscope in Pisces, Sagittarius rises in the ascendant. Sun rules the ninth house, and Moon rules the eighth house. In general, this combination is partly benefic and partly malefic here, though the malefic part is higher, in most cases. The concept of various planets exhibiting tendencies to be benefic or malefic on the basis of the houses they rule in a horoscope has been explained in the book 'Gemstones: Magic or Science?'.

Combination of Sun and combust Moon in the fourth house of horoscope in Pisces is malefic in many cases, though it may turn benefic in some cases. It may happen when such combination is influenced by one or more benefic planets, and/or an overall benefic horoscope. The concept of a malefic planet turning benefic due to influences of benefic planets has been explained in the book 'Match Making and Manglik Dosh'.

When benefic in nature, combination of Sun and combust Moon in the fourth house of a horoscope in Pisces can bless the native with good results related to father, mother, creativity, spiritual growth, lifespan, education, wealth, properties, vehicles, profession, finances, reputation, authority, recognition, fame and several other good results, depending on his/her overall horoscope and running times.

Such combination of Sun and combust Moon can render various types of benefits to the native, related to or through his father, mother and/or lifespan. Considering parents, native's father/mother may be a rich man/woman, a celebrity, an officer in government or a powerful politician. The native may enjoy many benefits because of his father/mother's money, influence and/or status. He/she may give a big amount of money, and/or wealth to the native, while he/she's alive, and/or through his/her will. Such combination of Sun and combust Moon can bless the native with good education, vehicles, residential house/houses and/or several other good results.

Looking at profession, such combust Moon can help the native achieve success as a fire fighter, fitness trainer, body builder, sportsman, athlete, physician, dietician, lawyer, astrologer, tantric, psychic, spiritual guru, healer, religious guru, teacher, preacher, consultant, researcher, analyst, host, artist, poet, chef, interior designer, professional dealing in education industry, coaching, food, health, pharma, medical, nursing, homecare, real estate, agriculture, hospitality, beauty, fashion, finance, television, music, sports, media, book, publishing, fitness, travel, hotel, airline, fishing, shipping, telecom, computer, software, IT, internet industry or some other type of professional, depending on his/her overall horoscope and running times.

Such combust Moon can help the native achieve success through a creative field as an actor, singer, musician, writer,

dancer, sportsman, artist, architect, designer, developer or some other likewise professional. Taking an example, suppose combust Moon is placed in the fourth house of a horoscope in Pisces with benefic Sun and benefic debilitated Mercury. Venus is placed in the second house in Capricorn, Mars is placed in the eighth house in Cancer, benefic Rahu is placed in the third house in Aquarius, and benefic retrograde Saturn is placed in the ninth house in Leo with Ketu. Sun and Mercury form Budhaditya Yoga in the fourth house. In this case, the native may become a music composer, and he may witness good results.

If benefic Jupiter is placed in the seventh house in Gemini, the equation may become better. The native may possess remarkable talent, and he may come across very good amount of success, money, recognition and fame. He may compose music for several hit songs, and he may receive many awards. He may also write some songs. If the finer factors and running times are supportive, he may become one of the most successful music composers of his time, and his net worth may be in multimillions.

Such combust Moon can bless the native with authority in government as a police officer, army, air force, naval, revenue, administrative, foreign services officer, judge, doctor, scientist, engineer, politician or some other type of professional. Taking an example, suppose combust Moon is placed in the fourth house of a horoscope in Pisces with retrograde Venus and benefic Sun. Benefic Mercury is placed in the third house in Aquarius, benefic Saturn is placed in the tenth house in Virgo, benefic Rahu is placed in the eighth house in Cancer, Ketu is placed in the second house in Capricorn, and Mars is placed in the eleventh house in Libra. In this case, the native may become an officer in revenue services, and he may enjoy a good career.

If benefic Jupiter is placed in the third house in Aquarius with Mercury; the equation may become better. In this case, the native may achieve success in civil exams, and he may get selected for the highest possible direct rank in revenue services. He may serve at several important posts during his career, and he may come across very good amount of success, recognition and authority. If the finer factors and running times are supportive, he may serve at one of the top 2 ranks in revenue services, before retirement.

On the other hand, when malefic in nature, combination of Sun and combust Moon in the fourth house of a horoscope in Pisces can trouble the native with problems related to father, mother, lifespan, education, wealth, properties, vehicles, profession, finances, reputation, authority, recognition and several other problems, depending on his/her overall horoscope and running times.

Sun rules the ninth house, Moon rules the eighth house, and they are placed in the fourth house. If such combination of Sun and combust Moon is influenced by malefic planets, and/or an overall malefic horoscope, the native may witness various types of problems related to or through his father, mother and/or lifespan. Considering parents, the native may not have a good equation with his father/mother, his parents may get divorced and he may live with his father/mother, his father/mother may suffer from a long-lasting illness, he/she may be an alcoholic and/or a drug addict, he/she may be a criminal, and/or he/she may die before native's age of 20, depending on native's overall horoscope and running times. He may also witness various types of problems related to properties, vehicles and/or mental health. Considering lifespan, the native may witness reduction in lifespan due to several reasons. For example, the native may die in an accident, through a natural disaster, due to a fatal disease, due to a fatal viral infection like COVID, due to drug addiction, he may commit suicide, or someone may kill him intentionally or unintentionally.

The native may witness delays, financial losses, setbacks, failures, job loss, bad reputation and several other problems related to or through his profession. Taking an example, suppose malefic combust Moon is placed in the fourth house of a horoscope in Pisces with Sun, malefic exalted Venus and malefic debilitated Rahu. Malefic debilitated Ketu is placed in the tenth house in Virgo with Saturn; Mars is placed in the third house in Aquarius, Mercury is placed in the fifth house in Aries, and retrograde Jupiter is placed in the twelfth house in Scorpio. Grahan Yoga is formed in the fourth house.

In this case, native's father may die before native's age of 15 or 10. His mother may get married again, but the native may not have a good equation with his stepfather as well as with his mother. He may not achieve much professional success till his age of 35/40, or throughout his life, though he may earn well at times. He may remain jobless for periods of more than 3 months, many times in his life. He may witness 1 or 2 failed marriages. He may die before his age of 60 or 55, due to some type of cancer, another fatal disease, in an accident, or because of a fatal viral infection like COVID.

Combust Moon in Fifth House in Aries

When Sun and combust Moon are placed in the fifth house of a horoscope in Aries, Sagittarius rises in the ascendant. Sun rules the ninth house, and Moon rules the eighth house. In general, this combination is partly benefic and partly malefic here, though the benefic part is higher, in most cases. The concept of various planets exhibiting tendencies to be benefic or malefic on the basis of the houses they rule in a horoscope has been explained in the book 'Gemstones: Magic or Science?'.

Combination of Sun and combust Moon in the fifth house of horoscope in Aries is benefic in many cases, though it may turn malefic in some cases. It may happen when such combination is influenced by one or more malefic planets, and/or an overall malefic horoscope. The concept of a benefic planet turning malefic due to influences of malefic planets has been explained in the book 'Match Making and Manglik Dosh'.

When benefic in nature, combination of Sun and combust Moon in the fifth house of a horoscope in Aries can bless the native with good results related to father, mother, lifespan, love life, children, creativity, spiritual growth, profession, finances, reputation, authority, recognition, fame and several other good results, depending on his/her overall horoscope and running times.

Such combination of Sun and combust Moon can render various types of benefits to the native, related to or through his father, mother and/or children. Considering parents, native's father/mother may be a rich man/woman, a celebrity, an officer in government or a powerful politician. The native may enjoy many benefits because of his father/mother's money, influence and/or status. He/she may give a big amount of money, and/or wealth to the native, while he/she's alive, and/or through his/her will. Considering children, the native may have children who may be physically, intellectually, emotionally, creatively and/or spiritually better or much better than average. Such children may achieve a lot in many spheres of their lives, and they may bring good name and many other good results to the native.

Looking at profession, such combust Moon can help the native achieve success as a fire fighter, fitness trainer, body builder, sportsman, athlete, physician, dietician, lawyer, astrologer, tantric, psychic, spiritual guru, healer, religious guru, teacher, preacher, consultant, researcher, analyst, host, artist, poet, chef, interior designer, police officer, army, air force, naval, revenue, administrative, foreign services officer, judge, doctor, scientist, engineer, politician, professional dealing in education industry, coaching, food, health, pharma, medical, nursing, homecare, real estate, agriculture, hospitality, beauty, fashion, finance, television, music, sports, media, book, publishing, fitness, travel, hotel, airline, fishing, shipping, telecom, computer, software, IT, internet industry

or some other type of professional, depending on his/her overall horoscope and running times.

Taking an example, suppose combust Moon is placed in the fifth house of a horoscope in Aries with benefic Mercury and benefic exalted Sun. Benefic retrograde Jupiter is placed in the ninth house in Leo, benefic Saturn is placed in the seventh house in Gemini with benefic Rahu; Ketu is placed in the first house in Sagittarius, and exalted Venus is placed in the fourth house in Pisces with Mars. Sun and Mercury form Budhaditya Yoga in the fifth house.

In this case, the native may start a company which may manufacture various types of liquor products, and he may come across very good amount of success, money and recognition. His business may expand after his age of 35/40, and it may keep growing. If the finer factors and running times are supportive, he may own a business empire worth in billions, by his age of 55/60.

Such combust Moon can help the native achieve success as an actor, singer, musician, writer, dancer, sportsman, artist, architect, designer, developer or some other likewise professional. Taking an example, suppose combust Moon is placed in the fifth house of a horoscope in Aries with Venus, benefic Mercury and benefic exalted Sun. Benefic Jupiter is placed in the eleventh house in Libra with Mars; benefic retrograde Saturn is placed in the tenth house in Virgo, benefic exalted Rahu is placed in the sixth house in Taurus, and exalted Ketu is placed in the twelfth house in Scorpio. Budhaditya Yoga is formed in the fifth house.

In this case, the native may become a professional cricketer (batsman). He may possess remarkable talent related to the sport, and he may come across very good amount of success, money, recognition and fame. He may deliver several match-winning performances, and he may receive many awards/medals. If the finer factors and running times are supportive, he may become one of the most successful batsmen of his time, and his net worth may be in multimillions.

On the other hand, when malefic in nature, combination of Sun and combust Moon in the fifth house of a horoscope in Aries can trouble the native with problems related to father, mother, lifespan, love life, children, profession, finances, reputation, authority, recognition and several other problems, depending on his/her overall horoscope and running times.

Sun rules the ninth house, Moon rules the eighth house, and they are placed in the fifth house. If such combination of Sun and combust Moon is influenced by malefic planets, and/or an overall malefic horoscope, the native may witness various types of problems related to or through his father, mother, children and/or lifespan. Considering parents, the native may not have a good equation with his father/mother, his parents may get divorced and he may live with his father/mother, his father/mother may suffer from a long-lasting illness, he/she may be an alcoholic and/or a drug addict, he/she may be a criminal, and/or he/she may die before native's age of 20, depending on native's overall horoscope and running times. Considering children, the native may lose one or more children through miscarriages that his wife may witness. He may witness delay in childbirth, and/or he may have children who may be physically and/or mentally troubled in some way. He may lose his children through divorce, or his children may engage in immoral/illegal activities, and he may witness bad reputation and many other problems because of them. Considering lifespan, the native may witness reduction in lifespan due to several reasons. For example, the native may die in an accident, through a natural disaster, due to a fatal disease, due to a fatal viral infection like COVID, due to drug addiction, he may commit suicide, or someone may kill him intentionally or unintentionally.

The native may witness delays, financial losses, setbacks, failures, job loss, bad reputation and several other problems related to or through his profession. Taking an example, suppose malefic combust Moon is placed in the fifth house of a horoscope in Aries with exalted Sun and malefic Venus. Malefic debilitated Ketu is placed in the sixth house in Taurus with Mercury and Saturn; and malefic debilitated Rahu is placed in the twelfth house in Scorpio with Mars and retrograde Jupiter. Angarak Yoga and Guru Chandal Yoga are formed in the twelfth house.

In this case, native's father as well as mother may die before his age of 20 or 15. He may not achieve much professional success till his age of 35/40, or throughout his life, though he may earn well at times. He may remain jobless for periods of more than 3 months, many times in his life. He may witness 1 or 2 failed marriages. He may lose one or more children to death, through miscarriages that his wife/wives may witness. He may die before his age of 60 or 55, due to a heart attack, in an accident, because of a fatal viral infection like COVID, or someone may kill him.

Combust Moon in Fifth House in Taurus

When Sun and combust Moon are placed in the fifth house of a horoscope in Taurus, Capricorn rises in the ascendant. Sun rules the eighth house, and Moon rules the seventh house. In general, this combination is partly benefic and partly malefic here, though the benefic part is higher, in most cases. The concept of various planets exhibiting tendencies to be benefic or malefic on the basis of the houses they rule in a horoscope has been explained in the book 'Gemstones: Magic or Science?'.

Combination of Sun and combust Moon in the fifth house of horoscope in Taurus is benefic in many cases, though it may turn malefic in some cases. It may happen when such combination is influenced by one or more malefic planets, and/or an overall malefic horoscope. The concept of a benefic planet turning malefic due to influences of malefic planets has been explained in the book 'Match Making and Manglik Dosh'.

When benefic in nature, combination of Sun and combust Moon in the fifth house of a horoscope in Taurus can bless the native with good results related to father, mother, marriage, husband, wife, lifespan, love life, children, creativity, spiritual growth, profession, finances, reputation, authority, recognition, fame and several other good results, depending on his/her overall horoscope and running times.

Such combination of Sun and combust Moon can render various types of benefits to the native, related to or through his father, mother, children and/or marriage. Considering parents, native's father/mother may be a rich man/woman, a celebrity, an officer in government or a powerful politician. The native may enjoy many benefits because of his father/ mother's money, influence and/or status. Considering children, the native may have children who may be physically, intellectually, emotionally, creatively and/or spiritually better or much better than average. Such children may achieve a lot in many spheres of their lives, and they may bring good name and many other good results to the native. Considering marriage, the native may get married to a woman who may be beautiful, rich, a celebrity, an officer in government, a powerful politician, a successful businesswoman, and/ or a citizen of a foreign country. The native may witness several benefits due to or through his wife and/or her family members.

Looking at profession, such combust Moon can help the native achieve success as a fire fighter, fitness trainer, body builder, sportsman, athlete, physician, dietician, lawyer, astrologer, tantric, psychic, spiritual guru, healer, religious guru, teacher, preacher, consultant, actor, singer, musician, writer, dancer, sportsman, artist, architect, designer, developer, poet, chef, interior designer, host, researcher, analyst, professional dealing in education industry, coaching, food, health, pharma, medical, nursing, homecare, real estate, agriculture, hospitality, beauty, fashion, finance, television, music, sports, media, book, publishing, fitness, travel, hotel, airline, fishing, shipping, telecom, computer, software, IT, internet industry or some other type of professional, depending on his/her overall horoscope and running times.

Taking an example, suppose benefic combust Moon is placed in the fifth house of a horoscope in Taurus with Sun, retrograde Mercury and benefic Venus. Benefic Mars is placed in the twelfth house in Sagittarius, benefic Rahu is placed in the eighth house in Leo, Ketu is placed in the second house in Aquarius, Jupiter is placed in the sixth house in Gemini, and benefic Saturn is placed in the ninth house in Virgo.

In this case, the native may become a scientist. He may specialize in nuclear science. He may possess remarkable knowledge of his field, and he may come across very good amount of success, recognition and authority, along with good amount of money. He may engage in research, and he may come across discoveries. He may receive awards as well as financial rewards. If the finer factors and running times are supportive, he may serve as the head of his department for several years.

Such combust Moon can bless the native with authority in government as a police officer, army, air force, naval, revenue, administrative, foreign services officer, judge, doctor, scientist, engineer, politician or some other type of professional. Taking an example, suppose benefic combust Moon is placed in the fifth house of a horoscope in Taurus with Sun and Mercury. Benefic Venus is placed in the sixth house in Gemini, benefic Mars forms Ruchaka Yoga in the fourth house in Aries, benefic Rahu is placed in the first house in Capricorn, Ketu is placed in the seventh house in Cancer with exalted Jupiter; and exalted Saturn forms Shasha Yoga in the tenth house in Libra.

In this case, the native may achieve success in competitive exams, and he may get selected for the highest possible direct rank in army. He may serve at several important posts, and he may come across very good amount of success, recognition and authority. If the finer factors and running times are supportive, he may serve at one of the top 2 ranks in army, before retirement.

On the other hand, when malefic in nature, combination of Sun and combust Moon in the fifth house of a horoscope in Taurus can trouble the native with problems related to father, mother, marriage, husband, wife, lifespan, love life, children, profession, finances, reputation, authority, recognition and several other problems, depending on his/her overall horoscope and running times.

Sun rules the eighth house, Moon rules the seventh house, and they are placed in the fifth house. If such combination of Sun and combust Moon is influenced by malefic planets, and/or an overall malefic horoscope, the native may witness various types of problems related to or through his father, mother, children, marriage and/or lifespan. Considering parents, the native may not have a good equation with his father/mother, his parents may get divorced and he may live with his father/mother, his father/mother may suffer from a long-lasting illness, he/she may be an alcoholic and/or a drug addict, he/she may be a criminal, and/or he/she may die before native's age of 20, depending on native's overall horoscope and running times. Considering children, the native may lose one or more children through miscarriages that his wife may witness. He may witness delay in childbirth, and/or he may have children who may be physically and/

or mentally troubled in some way. He may lose his children through divorce, or his children may engage in immoral/illegal activities, and he may witness bad reputation and many other problems because of them. Considering marriage, the native may witness delay/disturbances in marriage, and/or one or more failed marriages. Considering lifespan, the native may witness reduction in lifespan due to several reasons.

The native may witness delays, financial losses, setbacks, failures, job loss, bad reputation and several other problems related to or through his profession. Taking an example, suppose combust Moon is placed in the fifth house of a horoscope in Taurus with malefic Sun, malefic exalted Rahu and malefic Jupiter. Malefic exalted Ketu is placed in the eleventh house in Scorpio with retrograde Mars; retrograde Venus is placed in the sixth house in Gemini with Mercury; and retrograde Saturn is placed in the twelfth house in Sagittarius. Grahan Yoga and Guru Chandal Yoga are formed in the fifth house.

In this case, native's father may die before native's age of 10/5, and his mother may die before his age of 20/15. He may not find a permanent profession till his age of 35/40, or throughout his life, and he may only find temporary jobs. He may remain jobless for periods of more than 3 months, many times in his life. He may not get married till his age of 35/40, or throughout his life. He may not have a child till his age of 40/45, or throughout his life. He may die before his age of 55/50, due to a heart attack, some type of cancer, another fatal disease, or because of a fatal viral infection like COVID.

Combust Moon in Fifth House in Gemini

When Sun and combust Moon are placed in the fifth house of a horoscope in Gemini, Aquarius rises in the ascendant. Sun rules the seventh house, and Moon rules the sixth house. In general, this combination is partly benefic and partly malefic here, though the benefic part is higher, in most cases. The concept of various planets exhibiting tendencies to be benefic or malefic on the basis of the houses they rule in a horoscope has been explained in the book 'Gemstones: Magic or Science?'.

Combination of Sun and combust Moon in the fifth house of horoscope in Gemini is benefic in many cases, though it may turn malefic in some cases. It may happen when such combination is influenced by one or more malefic planets, and/or an overall malefic horoscope. The concept of a benefic planet turning malefic due to influences of malefic planets has been explained in the book 'Match Making and Manglik Dosh'.

When benefic in nature, combination of Sun and combust Moon in the fifth house of a horoscope in Gemini can bless the native with good results related to father, mother, marriage, husband, wife, love life, children, creativity, spiritual growth, profession, finances, reputation, authority, recognition, fame and several other good results, depending on his/her overall horoscope and running times.

Such combination of Sun and combust Moon can render various types of benefits to the native, related to or through his father, mother, children and/or marriage. Considering parents, native's father/mother may be a rich man/woman, a celebrity, an officer in government or a powerful politician. The native may enjoy many benefits because of his father/ mother's money, influence and/or status. He/she may give a big amount of money, and/or wealth to the native, while he/she's alive, and/or through his/her will. Considering children, the native may have children who may be physically, intellectually, emotionally, creatively and/or spiritually better or much better than average. Such children may achieve a lot in many spheres of their lives, and they may bring good name and many other good results to the native. Considering marriage, the native may get married to a woman who may be beautiful, rich, a celebrity, an officer in government, a powerful politician, a successful businesswoman, and/ or a citizen of a foreign country. The native may witness several benefits due to or through his wife and/or her family members.

Looking at profession, such combust Moon can help the native achieve success as a fire fighter, fitness trainer, body builder, sportsman, athlete, physician, dietician, lawyer, astrologer, tantric, psychic, spiritual guru, healer, religious guru, teacher, preacher, consultant, researcher, analyst, host, artist, poet, chef, interior designer, police officer, army, air force, naval, revenue, administrative, foreign services officer, judge, doctor, scientist, engineer, politician, professional dealing in education industry, coaching, food, health, pharma, medical, nursing, homecare, real estate, agriculture, hospitality, beauty, fashion, finance, television, music, sports, media, book, publishing, fitness, travel, hotel, airline, fishing, shipping, telecom, computer, software, IT, internet industry or some other type of professional, depending on his/her overall horoscope and running times.

Taking an example, suppose combust Moon is placed in the fifth house of a horoscope in Gemini with Mercury, benefic Sun and benefic Venus. Benefic debilitated Mars is placed in the sixth house in Cancer, benefic Jupiter is placed in the ninth house in Libra, Saturn is placed in the eighth house in Virgo, benefic Rahu is placed in the seventh house in Leo, and Ketu is placed in the first house in Aquarius.

In this case, the native may become a doctor. He may specialize in cardiology. He may possess remarkable knowledge of his field, and he may come across very good amount of success, money and recognition. If the finer factors and running times are supportive, he may become one of the most recognized cardiologists of his country, and his net worth may be in multimillions.

Such combust Moon can help the native achieve success through a creative field as an actor, singer, musician, writer, dancer, sportsman, artist, architect, designer, developer or some other likewise professional. Taking an example, suppose combust Moon is placed in the fifth house of a horoscope in Gemini with benefic Sun and benefic Venus. Mercury is placed in the fourth house in Taurus with Saturn; benefic Jupiter is placed in the ninth house in Libra with benefic Mars; benefic exalted Rahu is placed in the eighth house in Virgo, and exalted Ketu is placed in the second house in Pisces.

In this case, the native may write fictional books. He may possess remarkable writing talent, and he may come across very good amount of success, money, recognition and fame. He may write in several genres including science-fiction, mystery and adventure. He may deliver several bestsellers, and he may receive many awards. If the finer factors and running times are supportive, he may become one of the most successful writers of his time, and his net worth may be in multimillions.

On the other hand, when malefic in nature, combination of Sun and combust Moon in the fifth house of a horoscope in Gemini can trouble the native with problems related to father, mother, marriage, husband, wife, love life, children, profession, finances, reputation, authority, recognition and several other problems, depending on his/her overall horoscope and running times.

Sun rules the seventh house, Moon rules the sixth house, and they are placed in the fifth house. If such combination of Sun and combust Moon is influenced by malefic planets, and/or an overall malefic horoscope, the native may witness various types of problems related to or through his father, mother, children and/or marriage. Considering parents, the native may not have a good equation with his father/mother, his parents may get divorced and he may live with his father/mother, his father/mother may suffer from a long-lasting illness, he/she may be an alcoholic and/or a drug addict, he/she may be a criminal, and/or he/she may die before native's age of 20, depending on native's overall horoscope and running times. Considering children, the native may lose one or more children through miscarriages that his wife may witness. He may witness delay in childbirth, and/or he may have children who may be physically and/or mentally troubled in some way. He may lose his children through divorce, or his children may engage in immoral/illegal activities, and he may witness bad reputation and many other problems because of them. Considering marriage, the native may witness delay/disturbances in marriage, and/or one or more failed marriages. He may have serious differences of opinion with his wife, she may suffer from a long-lasting illness, she may be an alcoholic and/or a drug addict, she may be a criminal, she may not be loyal to him, she may have extramarital affair/affairs, and/or she may die within 10 or 5 years of marriage.

The native may witness delays, financial losses, setbacks, failures, job loss, bad reputation and several other problems related to or through his profession. Taking an example, suppose malefic combust Moon is placed in the fifth house of a horoscope in Gemini with Sun, Mercury and malefic Rahu. Malefic Ketu is placed in the eleventh house in Sagittarius with Mars; Venus is placed in the sixth house in Cancer with retrograde Saturn; and benefic Jupiter is placed in the seventh house in Leo. Grahan Yoga is formed in the fifth house.

In this case, native's father may die before native's age of 10 or 5, and native's mother may die before his age of 20 or 15. He may not find a permanent profession throughout his life, and he may only find temporary jobs, through he may earn well at times. He may remain jobless for periods of more than 3 months, many times in his life. He may witness 1 or 2 failed marriages. He may lose one or more children to death, through miscarriages that his wife/wives may witness.

Combust Moon in Fifth House in Cancer

When Sun and combust Moon are placed in the fifth house of a horoscope in Cancer, Pisces rises in the ascendant. Sun rules the sixth house, and Moon rules the fifth house. In general, this combination is partly benefic and partly malefic here, though the benefic part is higher, in most cases. The concept of various planets exhibiting tendencies to be benefic or malefic on the basis of the houses they rule in a horoscope has been explained in the book 'Gemstones: Magic or Science?'.

Combination of Sun and combust Moon in the fifth house of horoscope in Cancer is benefic in many cases, though it may turn malefic in some cases. It may happen when such combination is influenced by one or more malefic planets, and/or an overall malefic horoscope. The concept of a benefic planet turning malefic due to influences of malefic planets has been explained in the book 'Match Making and Manglik Dosh'.

When benefic in nature, combination of Sun and combust Moon in the fifth house of a horoscope in Cancer can bless the native with good results related to father, mother, love life, children, creativity, spiritual growth, profession, finances, reputation, authority, recognition, fame and several other good results, depending on his/her overall horoscope and running times.

Such combination of Sun and combust Moon can render various types of benefits to the native, related to or through his father, mother and/or children. Considering parents, native's father/mother may be a rich man/woman, a celebrity, an officer in government or a powerful politician. The native may enjoy many benefits because of his father/ mother's money, influence and/or status. He/she may give a big amount of money, and/or wealth to the native, while he/she's alive, and/or through his/her will. Considering children, the native may have children who may be physically, intellectually, emotionally, creatively and/or spiritually better or much better than average. Such children may achieve a lot in many spheres of their lives, and they may bring good name and many other good results to the native.

Looking at profession, such combust Moon can help the native achieve success as a fire fighter, fitness trainer, body builder, sportsman, athlete, physician, dietician, lawyer, astrologer, tantric, psychic, spiritual guru, healer, religious guru, teacher, preacher, consultant, researcher, analyst, host, artist, poet, chef, interior designer, police officer, army, air force, naval, revenue, administrative, foreign services officer, judge, doctor, scientist, engineer, politician, professional dealing in education industry, coaching, food, health, pharma, medical, nursing, homecare, real estate, agriculture, hospitality, beauty, fashion, finance, television, music, sports, media, book, publishing, fitness, travel, hotel, airline, fishing, shipping, telecom, computer, software, IT, internet industry

or some other type of professional, depending on his/her overall horoscope and running times.

Taking an example, suppose benefic combust Moon is placed in the fifth house of a horoscope in Cancer with Sun. Benefic Mars is placed in the sixth house in Leo with Venus and Ketu; benefic Rahu is placed in the twelfth house in Aquarius, benefic Jupiter is placed in the fourth house in Gemini with benefic Mercury; and exalted Saturn is placed in the eighth house in Libra. Mercury forms Bhadra Yoga in the fourth house.

In this case, the native may become a mathematician. He may possess remarkable knowledge of his field, and he may come across very good amount of success and recognition, along with good amount of money. He may conduct research, and he may come across important theories. He may write several books on various topics, and he may come across money, recognition and fame through them. If the finer factors and running times are supportive, he may become one of the top mathematicians of his time, and his net worth may be in multimillions.

Such combust Moon can help the native achieve success through a creative field as an actor, singer, musician, writer, dancer, sportsman, artist, architect, designer, developer or some other likewise professional. Taking an example, suppose benefic combust Moon is placed in the fifth house of a horoscope in Cancer with Sun and benefic retrograde Mercury. Venus is placed in the fourth house in Gemini, benefic Jupiter is placed in the third house in Taurus with benefic exalted Rahu; benefic Mars is placed in the ninth house in Scorpio with exalted Ketu; and Saturn is placed in the seventh house in Virgo.

In this case, the native may become a music composer. He may possess remarkable talent, and he may come across very good amount of success, money, recognition and fame. He may also write some songs, and he may sing some songs. He may compose music for several hit songs, and he may receive many awards. If the finer factors and running times are supportive, he may become one of the most successful music composers of his time, and his net worth may be in multimillions.

On the other hand, when malefic in nature, combination of Sun and combust Moon in the fifth house of a horoscope in Cancer can trouble the native with problems related to father, mother, love life, children, profession, finances, reputation, authority, recognition and several other problems, depending on his/her overall horoscope and running times.

Sun rules the sixth house, Moon rules the fifth house, and they are placed in the fifth house. If such combination of Sun and combust Moon is influenced by malefic planets, and/or an overall malefic horoscope, the native may witness various types of problems related to or through his father, mother and/or children. Considering parents, the native may not have a good equation with his father/mother, his parents may get divorced and he may live with his father/ mother, his father/mother may suffer from a long-lasting illness, he/she may be an alcoholic and/or a drug addict, he/she may be a criminal, and/or he/she may die before native's age of 20, depending on native's overall horoscope and running times. Considering children, the native may lose one or more children through miscarriages that his wife may witness. He may witness delay in childbirth, and/or he may have children who may be physically and/or mentally

troubled in some way. He may lose his children through divorce, or his children may engage in immoral/illegal activities, and he may witness bad reputation and many other problems because of them.

The native may witness delays, financial losses, setbacks, failures, job loss, bad reputation and several other problems related to or through his profession. Taking an example, suppose combust Moon is placed in the fifth house of a horoscope in Cancer with malefic Sun and malefic Venus. Malefic Rahu is placed in the sixth house in Leo with Mercury; malefic Ketu is placed in the twelfth house in Aquarius with Mars; and malefic exalted Saturn is placed in the eighth house in Libra with Jupiter.

In this case, native's father may die before native's age of 15 or 10. The native may not have a good equation with his mother. He may not achieve much professional success till his age of 35/40, or throughout his life. He may witness financial tightness and debts, many times in his life. He may remain jobless for periods of more than 6 months, many times in his life. He may witness 1 or 2 failed marriages. He may lose one or more children to death, through miscarriages that his wife/wives may witness.

Combust Moon in Fifth House in Leo

When Sun and combust Moon are placed in the fifth house of a horoscope in Leo, Aries rises in the ascendant. Sun rules the fifth house, and Moon rules the fourth house. In general, this combination is benefic here, in most cases. The concept of various planets exhibiting tendencies to be benefic or malefic on the basis of the houses they rule in a horoscope has been explained in the book 'Gemstones: Magic or Science?'.

Combination of Sun and combust Moon in the fifth house of horoscope in Leo is benefic in most cases, though it may turn malefic in some cases. It may happen when such combination is influenced by one or more malefic planets, and/or an overall malefic horoscope. The concept of a benefic planet turning malefic due to influences of malefic planets has been explained in the book 'Match Making and Manglik Dosh'.

When benefic in nature, combination of Sun and combust Moon in the fifth house of a horoscope in Leo can bless the native with good results related to father, mother, education, wealth, properties, vehicles, love life, children, creativity, spiritual growth, profession, finances, reputation, authority, recognition, fame and several other good results, depending on his/her overall horoscope and running times.

Such combination of Sun and combust Moon can render various types of benefits to the native, related to or through his father, mother and/or children. Considering parents, native's father/mother may be a rich man/woman, a celebrity, an officer in government or a powerful politician. The native may enjoy many benefits because of his father/mother's money, influence and/or status. He/she may give a big amount of money, and/or wealth to the native, while he/she's alive, and/or through his/her will. Considering children, the native may have children who may be physically, intellectually, emotionally, creatively and/or spiritually better or much better than average. Such children may achieve a lot in many spheres of their lives, and they may bring good name and many other good results to the native.

Looking at profession, such combust Moon can help the native achieve success as a fire fighter, fitness trainer, body builder, sportsman, athlete, physician, dietician, lawyer, astrologer, tantric, psychic, spiritual guru, healer, religious guru, teacher, preacher, consultant, researcher, analyst, host, artist, poet, chef, interior designer, police officer, army, air force, naval, revenue, administrative, foreign services officer, judge, doctor, scientist, engineer, politician, professional dealing in education industry, coaching, food, health, pharma, medical, nursing, homecare, real estate, agriculture, hospitality, beauty, fashion, finance, television, music, sports, media, book, publishing, fitness, travel, hotel, airline, fishing, shipping, telecom, computer, software, IT, internet industry

or some other type of professional, depending on his/her overall horoscope and running times.

Such combust Moon can help the native achieve success as an actor, singer, musician, writer, dancer, sportsman, artist, architect, designer, developer or some other likewise professional. Taking an example, suppose benefic combust Moon is placed in the fifth house of a horoscope in Leo with Mercury, Mars, Jupiter and benefic Sun. Benefic retrograde Saturn is placed in the twelfth house in Pisces, benefic Rahu is placed in the third house in Gemini, and Ketu is placed in the ninth house in Sagittarius. In this case, the native may become a cricketer (batsman), and he may witness good results.

If benefic Venus is placed in the third house in Gemini with Rahu; the equation may become better. The native may possess remarkable talent related to the sport, and he may come across very good amount of success, money, recognition and fame. He may deliver several match-winning performances, and he may receive many awards/medals. If the finer factors and running times are supportive, he may become one of the greatest batsmen of all time, and his net worth may be in multimillions.

Taking another example, suppose benefic combust Moon is placed in the fifth house of a horoscope in Leo with retrograde Mercury and benefic Sun. Mars is placed in the seventh house in Libra, benefic debilitated Rahu is placed in the eighth house in Scorpio, debilitated Ketu is placed in the second house in Taurus, retrograde Jupiter is placed in the eleventh house in Aquarius, and benefic Venus is placed in the fourth house in Cancer. In this case, the native may become a tennis player, and he may witness good results.

If benefic Saturn is placed in the fourth house in Cancer with Venus; the equation may become better. The native may possess remarkable talent related to the sport, and he may come across very good amount of success, money, recognition and fame. He may win majority of his matches as well as several championship titles. He may rank among top players. If the finer factors and running times are supportive, he may become one of the most successful tennis players of his time, and his net worth may be in multimillions.

On the other hand, when malefic in nature, combination of Sun and combust Moon in the fifth house of a horoscope in Leo can trouble the native with problems related to father, mother, education, wealth, properties, vehicles, love life, children, profession, finances, reputation, authority, recognition and several other problems, depending on his/her overall horoscope and running times.

Sun rules the fifth house, Moon rules the fourth house, and they are placed in the fifth house. If such combination of Sun and combust Moon is influenced by malefic planets, and/or an overall malefic horoscope, the native may witness various types of problems related to or through his father, mother and/or children. Considering parents, the native may not have a good equation with his father/mother, his parents may get divorced and he may live with his father/mother, his father/mother may suffer from a long-lasting illness, he/she may be an alcoholic and/or a drug addict, he/she may be a criminal, and/or he/she may die before native's age of 20, depending on native's overall horoscope and running times. Considering children, the native may lose one or more children through miscarriages that his wife may witness. He may witness delay in childbirth, and/or he may have children who may be physically and/or mentally

troubled in some way. He may lose his children through divorce, or his children may engage in immoral/illegal activities, and he may witness bad reputation and many other problems because of them.

The native may witness delays, financial losses, setbacks, failures, job loss, bad reputation and several other problems related to or through his profession. Taking an example, suppose combust Moon is placed in the fifth house of a horoscope in Leo with Sun, Mars and malefic retrograde Mercury. Malefic Rahu is placed in the ninth house in Sagittarius, malefic Ketu is placed in the third house in Gemini, benefic Saturn is placed in the fourth house in Cancer, retrograde Jupiter is placed in the eighth house in Scorpio, and debilitated Venus is placed in the sixth house in Virgo.

In this case, native's father may die before native's age of 10 or 5. His mother may get married again, but the native may not have a good equation with his stepfather. The native may not achieve much professional success till his age of 35/40, or throughout his life. He may witness financial tightness and debts, many times in his life. He may witness 1 or 2 failed marriages. He may lose one or more children to death, through miscarriages that his wife/wives may witness.

Combust Moon in Fifth House in Virgo

When Sun and combust Moon are placed in the fifth house of a horoscope in Virgo, Taurus rises in the ascendant. Sun rules the fourth house, and Moon rules the third house. In general, this combination is benefic here, in most cases. The concept of various planets exhibiting tendencies to be benefic or malefic on the basis of the houses they rule in a horoscope has been explained in the book 'Gemstones: Magic or Science?'.

Combination of Sun and combust Moon in the fifth house of horoscope in Virgo is benefic in most cases, though it may turn malefic in some cases. It may happen when such combination is influenced by one or more malefic planets, and/or an overall malefic horoscope. The concept of a benefic planet turning malefic due to influences of malefic planets has been explained in the book 'Match Making and Manglik Dosh'.

When benefic in nature, combination of Sun and combust Moon in the fifth house of a horoscope in Virgo can bless the native with good results related to father, mother, education, wealth, properties, vehicles, siblings, colleagues, love life, children, creativity, spiritual growth, profession, finances, reputation, authority, recognition, fame and several other good results, depending on his/her overall horoscope and running times.

Such combination of Sun and combust Moon can render various types of benefits to the native, related to or through his father, mother, children and/or siblings. Considering parents, native's father/mother may be a rich man/woman, a celebrity, an officer in government or a powerful politician. The native may enjoy many benefits because of his father/ mother's money, influence and/or status. He/she may give a big amount of money, and/or wealth to the native, while he/she's alive, and/or through his/her will. Considering children, the native may have children who may be physically, intellectually, emotionally, creatively and/or spiritually better or much better than average. Considering siblings, some of them may stand by the native and they may help him get out of his problems, many times in his life.

Looking at profession, such combust Moon can help the native achieve success as a fire fighter, fitness trainer, body builder, sportsman, athlete, physician, dietician, lawyer, astrologer, tantric, psychic, spiritual guru, healer, religious guru, teacher, preacher, consultant, researcher, analyst, host, artist, poet, chef, interior designer, police officer, army, air force, naval, revenue, administrative, foreign services officer, judge, doctor, scientist, engineer, politician, professional dealing in education industry, coaching, food, health, pharma, medical, nursing, homecare, real estate, agriculture, hospitality, beauty, fashion, finance, television, music, sports, media, book, publishing, fitness, travel, hotel, airline, fishing, shipping, telecom, computer, software, IT, internet industry

or some other type of professional, depending on his/her overall horoscope and running times.

Such combust Moon can help the native achieve success through a creative field as an actor, singer, musician, writer, dancer, sportsman, artist, architect, designer, developer or some other likewise professional. Taking an example, suppose benefic combust Moon is placed in the fifth house of a horoscope in Virgo with debilitated Venus, benefic Sun and benefic exalted Mercury. Benefic exalted Rahu is placed in the first house in Taurus with Jupiter; exalted Ketu is placed in the seventh house in Scorpio, Mars is placed in the sixth house in Libra, and benefic Saturn is placed in the fourth house in Leo. Sun and Mercury form Budhaditya Yoga in the fifth house.

In this case, the native may become an actor. He may possess remarkable acting talent, and he may come across very good amount of success, money, recognition and fame. He may perform very well in the genres of drama, romance and comedy. He may deliver several hit movies, and he may receive many awards. If the finer factors and running times are supportive, he may become one of the most successful actors of his time, and his net worth may be in multimillions.

Taking another example, suppose benefic combust Moon is placed in the fifth house of a horoscope in Virgo with benefic Sun. Benefic Mercury is placed in the fourth house in Leo with benefic Saturn; Venus is placed in the third house in Cancer, benefic Rahu is placed in the second house in Gemini, Ketu is placed in the eighth house in Sagittarius, Mars is placed in the seventh house in Scorpio, and Jupiter is placed in the eleventh house in Pisces.

In this case, the native may become an architect. He may possess remarkable talent, and he may come across very good amount of success, money and recognition, along with good amount of fame. He may design several prestigious structures including parks, stadiums, residential and commercial complexes. If the finer factors and running times are supportive, he may become a well-recognized architect, and his net worth may be in multimillions.

On the other hand, when malefic in nature, combination of Sun and combust Moon in the fifth house of a horoscope in Virgo can trouble the native with problems related to father, mother, education, wealth, properties, vehicles, siblings, colleagues, love life, children, profession, finances, reputation, authority, recognition and several other problems, depending on his/her overall horoscope and running times.

Sun rules the fourth house, Moon rules the third house, and they are placed in the fifth house. If such combination of Sun and combust Moon is influenced by malefic planets, and/or an overall malefic horoscope, the native may witness various types of problems related to or through his father, mother, children and/or siblings. Considering parents, the native may not have a good equation with his father/mother, his parents may get divorced and he may live with his father/mother, his father/mother may suffer from a long-lasting illness, he/she may be an alcoholic and/or a drug addict, he/she may be a criminal, and/or he/she may die before native's age of 20, depending on native's overall horoscope and running times. Considering children, the native may lose one or more children through miscarriages that his wife may witness. He may witness delay in childbirth, and/or he may have children who may be physically and/or mentally troubled in some way. He may lose his children through divorce, or his children may engage in immoral/illegal activities, and he may witness bad reputation and many other problems because of them. Considering siblings, the native may have bad relationships with some of his siblings, and/or he may witness various types of problems through them or due to them. In an extreme case, the native may lose one or more siblings to death, before his age of 40 or 35.

The native may witness delays, financial losses, setbacks, failures, job loss, bad reputation and several other problems related to or through his profession. Taking an example, suppose combust Moon is placed in the fifth house of a horoscope in Virgo with Sun, malefic Mars and malefic Jupiter. Malefic Rahu is placed in the sixth house in Libra with Venus and Mercury; malefic Ketu is placed in the twelfth house in Aries, and Saturn is placed in the eighth house in Sagittarius.

In this case, native's mother may die before his age of 10 or 5, and his father may die before native's age of 20 or 15. The native may not find a permanent profession till his age of 35/40, or throughout his life, though he may earn well at times. He may witness financial losses and bad reputation through profession. He may lose one or more siblings to death, before his age of 35 or 30. He may witness 1 or 2 failed marriages. He may lose one or more children to death, through miscarriages that his wife/wives may witness. If the finer factors and running times are very bad for child aspect, he may not have an alive child, throughout his life.

Combust Moon in Fifth House in Libra

When Sun and combust Moon are placed in the fifth house of a horoscope in Libra, Gemini rises in the ascendant. Sun rules the third house, and Moon rules the second house. In general, this combination is benefic here, in most cases. The concept of various planets exhibiting tendencies to be benefic or malefic on the basis of the houses they rule in a horoscope has been explained in the book 'Gemstones: Magic or Science?'.

Combination of Sun and combust Moon in the fifth house of horoscope in Libra is benefic in most cases, though it may turn malefic in some cases. It may happen when such combination is influenced by one or more malefic planets, and/or an overall malefic horoscope. The concept of a benefic planet turning malefic due to influences of malefic planets has been explained in the book 'Match Making and Manglik Dosh'.

When benefic in nature, combination of Sun and combust Moon in the fifth house of a horoscope in Libra can bless the native with good results related to father, mother, family, wealth, speech, siblings, colleagues, love life, children, creativity, spiritual growth, profession, finances, reputation, authority, recognition, fame and several other good results, depending on his/her overall horoscope and running times.

Such combination of Sun and combust Moon can render various types of benefits to the native, related to or through his father, mother, children, siblings and/or family. Considering parents, native's father/mother may be a rich man/woman, a celebrity, an officer in government or a powerful politician. The native may enjoy many benefits because of his father/mother's money, influence and/or status. He/she may give a big amount of money, and/or wealth to the native, while he/she's alive, and/or through his/her will. Considering children, the native may have children who may be physically, intellectually, emotionally, creatively and/or spiritually better or much better than average. Considering siblings, some of them may stand by the native and they may help him get out of his problems, many times in his life.

Looking at profession, such combust Moon can help the native achieve success as a fire fighter, fitness trainer, body builder, sportsman, athlete, physician, dietician, lawyer, astrologer, tantric, psychic, spiritual guru, healer, religious guru, teacher, preacher, consultant, researcher, analyst, host, artist, poet, chef, interior designer, police officer, army, air force, naval, revenue, administrative, foreign services officer, judge, doctor, scientist, engineer, politician, professional dealing in education industry, coaching, food, health, pharma, medical, nursing, homecare, real estate, agriculture, hospitality, beauty, fashion, finance, television, music, sports, media, book, publishing, fitness, travel, hotel, airline, fishing, shipping, telecom, computer, software, IT, internet industry

or some other type of professional, depending on his/her overall horoscope and running times.

Such combust Moon can help the native achieve success through a creative field as an actor, singer, musician, writer, dancer, sportsman, artist, architect, designer, developer or some other likewise professional. Taking an example, suppose benefic combust Moon is placed in the fifth house of a horoscope in Libra with benefic Mercury and benefic debilitated Sun. Benefic exalted Jupiter is placed in the second house in Cancer with debilitated Mars; benefic Rahu is placed in the ninth house in Aquarius, Ketu is placed in the third house in Leo, and Venus is placed in the seventh house in Sagittarius with Saturn. Sun and Mercury form Budhaditya Yoga in the fifth house.

In this case, the native may become a singer. He may possess remarkable talent, and he may come across very good amount of success, money, recognition and fame. He may deliver several hit songs, and he may receive many awards. If the finer factors and running times are supportive, he may become one of the most successful singers of his time, and his net worth may be in multimillions.

Taking another example, suppose benefic combust Moon is placed in the fifth house of a horoscope in Libra with benefic debilitated Sun. Benefic exalted Mercury forms Bhadra Yoga in the fourth house in Virgo, benefic Rahu is placed in the third house in Leo with Saturn; benefic Jupiter is placed in the ninth house in Aquarius with Mars and Ketu; and Venus is placed in the sixth house in Scorpio.

In this case, the native may write fictional books. He may possess remarkable talent, and he may come across very good amount of success, money, recognition and fame.

He may write in several genres including science-fiction, extraterrestrial and war. He may deliver several bestsellers, and he may receive many awards. If the finer factors and running times are supportive, he may become one of the most successful writers of his time, and his net worth may be in multimillions.

On the other hand, when malefic in nature, combination of Sun and combust Moon in the fifth house of a horoscope in Libra can trouble the native with problems related to father, mother, family, wealth, speech, siblings, colleagues, love life, children, profession, finances, reputation, authority, recognition and several other problems, depending on his/her overall horoscope and running times.

Sun rules the third house, Moon rules the second house, and they are placed in the fifth house. If such combination of Sun and combust Moon is influenced by malefic planets, and/or an overall malefic horoscope, the native may witness various types of problems related to or through his father, mother, children, siblings and/or family. Considering parents, the native may not have a good equation with his father/mother, his parents may get divorced and he may live with his father/mother, his father/mother may suffer from a long-lasting illness, he/she may be an alcoholic and/or a drug addict, he/she may be a criminal, and/or he/she may die before native's age of 20, depending on native's overall horoscope and running times. Considering children, the native may lose one or more children through miscarriages that his wife may witness. He may witness delay in childbirth, and/or he may have children who may be physically and/or mentally troubled in some way. He may lose his children through divorce, or his children may engage in immoral/illegal activities, and he may witness bad reputation and many other problems because of them. Considering siblings, the native may have bad relationships with some of his siblings, and/or he may witness various types of problems through them or due to them. In an extreme case, the native may lose one or more siblings to death, before his age of 40 or 35.

The native may witness delays, financial losses, setbacks, failures, job loss, bad reputation and several other problems related to or through his profession. Taking an example, suppose combust Moon is placed in the fifth house of a horoscope in Libra with debilitated Sun, malefic Rahu and malefic Mars. Malefic Ketu is placed in the eleventh house in Aries, benefic exalted Mercury forms Bhadra Yoga in the fourth house in Virgo, Venus is placed in the sixth house in Scorpio with Jupiter; and retrograde Saturn is placed in the twelfth house in Taurus. Grahan Yoga and Angarak Yoga are formed in the fifth house.

In this case, native's father may die before native's age of 10 or 5. His mother may get married again, but the native may not have a good equation with his stepfather. The native may not find a permanent profession till his age of 35/40, or throughout his life, though he may earn well at times. He may remain jobless for periods of more than 3 months, many times in his life. He may lose one or more siblings to death, before his age of 35/30. He may witness 1 or 2 failed marriages. He may lose one or more children to death, through miscarriages that his wife/wives may witness.

Combust Moon in Fifth House in Scorpio

When Sun and combust Moon are placed in the fifth house of a horoscope in Scorpio, Cancer rises in the ascendant. Sun rules the second house, and Moon rules the first house. In general, this combination is benefic here, in most cases. The concept of various planets exhibiting tendencies to be benefic or malefic on the basis of the houses they rule in a horoscope has been explained in the book 'Gemstones: Magic or Science?'.

Combination of Sun and combust Moon in the fifth house of horoscope in Scorpio is benefic in most cases, though it may turn malefic in some cases. It may happen when such combination is influenced by one or more malefic planets, and/or an overall malefic horoscope. The concept of a benefic planet turning malefic due to influences of malefic planets has been explained in the book 'Match Making and Manglik Dosh'.

When benefic in nature, combination of Sun and combust Moon in the fifth house of a horoscope in Scorpio can bless the native with good results related to father, mother, health, lifespan, family, wealth, speech, love life, children, creativity, spiritual growth, profession, finances, reputation, authority, recognition, fame and several other good results, depending on his/her overall horoscope and running times.

Such combination of Sun and combust Moon can render various types of benefits to the native, related to or through his father, mother, children, family and/or lifespan. Considering parents, native's father/mother may be a rich man/woman, a celebrity, an officer in government or a powerful politician. The native may enjoy many benefits because of his father/mother's money, influence and/or status. He/she may give a big amount of money, and/or wealth to the native, while he/she's alive, and/or through his/her will. Considering children, the native may have children who may be physically, intellectually, emotionally, creatively and/or spiritually better or much better than average. Such children may achieve a lot in many spheres of their lives, and they may bring good name and many other good results to the native.

Looking at profession, such combust Moon can help the native achieve success as a fire fighter, fitness trainer, body builder, sportsman, athlete, physician, dietician, lawyer, astrologer, tantric, psychic, spiritual guru, healer, religious guru, teacher, preacher, consultant, researcher, analyst, host, artist, poet, chef, interior designer, police officer, army, air force, naval, revenue, administrative, foreign services officer, judge, doctor, scientist, engineer, politician, professional dealing in education industry, coaching, food, health, pharma, medical, nursing, homecare, real estate, agriculture, hospitality, beauty, fashion, finance, television, music, sports, media, book, publishing, fitness, travel, hotel, airline, fishing,

shipping, telecom, computer, software, IT, internet industry or some other type of professional, depending on his/her overall horoscope and running times.

Taking an example, suppose benefic combust Moon is placed in the fifth house of a horoscope in Scorpio with Mercury, benefic Venus, benefic Sun and benefic Mars. Benefic Rahu is placed in the second house in Leo, Ketu is placed in the eighth house in Aquarius, retrograde Jupiter is placed in the first house in Cancer, and retrograde Saturn is placed in the eleventh house in Taurus. Moon and Mars form Neechbhang Rajyoga as well as Chandra Mangal Yoga in the fifth house.

In this case, the native may start a company which may make various types of packed dairy and food products. He may come across very good amount of success, money and recognition. His business may expand after his age of 35/40, and it may keep growing. If the finer factors and running times are supportive, he may own a business empire worth in billions, by his age of 55/60.

Such combust Moon can help the native achieve success through a creative field as an actor, singer, musician, writer, dancer, sportsman, artist, architect, designer, developer or some other likewise professional. Taking an example for a female native, suppose benefic combust Moon is placed in the fifth house of a horoscope in Scorpio with Mercury and benefic Sun. Benefic Venus is placed in the fourth house in Libra with benefic Mars; benefic exalted Rahu is placed in the third house in Virgo, exalted Ketu is placed in the ninth house in Pisces with retrograde Saturn; and retrograde Jupiter is placed in the first house in Cancer. Venus forms Malavya Yoga in the fourth house.

In this case, the native may become an actor. She may possess remarkable talent, and she may come across very good amount of success, money, recognition and fame. She may perform very well in the genres of romance, drama and intense type of roles. She may deliver several hit movies, and she may receive many awards. If the finer factors and running times are supportive, she may become one of the most successful actors of her time, and her net worth may be in multimillions.

On the other hand, when malefic in nature, combination of Sun and combust Moon in the fifth house of a horoscope in Scorpio can trouble the native with problems related to father, mother, health, lifespan, family, wealth, speech, love life, children, profession, finances, reputation, authority, recognition and several other problems, depending on his/her overall horoscope and running times.

Sun rules the second house, Moon rules the first house, and they are placed in the fifth house. If such combination of Sun and combust Moon is influenced by malefic planets, and/or an overall malefic horoscope, the native may witness various types of problems related to or through his father, mother, children, family and/or lifespan. Considering parents, the native may not have a good equation with his father/mother, his parents may get divorced and he may live with his father/mother, his father/mother may suffer from a long-lasting illness, he/she may be an alcoholic and/or a drug addict, he/she may be a criminal, and/or he/she may die before native's age of 20, depending on native's overall horoscope and running times. Considering children, the native may lose one or more children through miscarriages that his wife may witness. He may witness delay in childbirth, and/or he may have children who may be physically and/

or mentally troubled in some way. He may lose his children through divorce, or his children may engage in immoral/ illegal activities, and he may witness bad reputation and many other problems because of them. Considering lifespan, the native may witness reduction in lifespan due to several reasons.

The native may witness delays, financial losses, setbacks, failures, job loss, bad reputation and several other problems related to or through his profession. Taking an example, suppose combust Moon is placed in the fifth house of a horoscope in Scorpio with Sun, malefic retrograde Mercury and malefic Saturn. Venus is placed in the sixth house in Sagittarius with Mars; malefic Rahu is placed in the fourth house in Libra with Jupiter; and malefic Ketu is placed in the tenth house in Aries. Guru Chandal Yoga is formed in the fourth house.

In this case, native's mother may die before his age of 10 or 5. His father may get married again, but the native may not have a good equation with his stepmother. He may not find a permanent profession till his age of 35/40, or throughout his life, though he may earn well at times. He may remain jobless for periods of more than 3 months, many times in his life. He may witness 1 or 2 failed marriages. He may lose his first wife to death. He may lose one or more children to death, through miscarriages that his wife/wives may witness. He may die before his age of 60 or 55, due to a heart attack, some type of fatal disease like cancer, or because of a fatal viral infection like COVID.

Combust Moon in Fifth House in Sagittarius

When Sun and combust Moon are placed in the fifth house of a horoscope in Sagittarius, Leo rises in the ascendant. Sun rules the first house, and Moon rules the twelfth house. In general, this combination is partly benefic and partly malefic here, though the benefic part is higher, in most cases. The concept of various planets exhibiting tendencies to be benefic or malefic on the basis of the houses they rule in a horoscope has been explained in the book 'Gemstones: Magic or Science?'.

Combination of Sun and combust Moon in the fifth house of horoscope in Sagittarius is benefic in many cases, though it may turn malefic in some cases. It may happen when such combination is influenced by one or more malefic planets, and/or an overall malefic horoscope. The concept of a benefic planet turning malefic due to influences of malefic planets has been explained in the book 'Match Making and Manglik Dosh'.

When benefic in nature, combination of Sun and combust Moon in the fifth house of a horoscope in Sagittarius can bless the native with good results related to father, mother, health, lifespan, love life, children, creativity, spiritual growth, profession, finances, reputation, authority, recognition, fame and several other good results, depending on his/her overall horoscope and running times.

Such combination of Sun and combust Moon can render various types of benefits to the native, related to or through his father, mother, children and/or lifespan. Considering parents, native's father/mother may be a rich man/woman, a celebrity, an officer in government or a powerful politician. The native may enjoy many benefits because of his father/mother's money, influence and/or status. He/she may give a big amount of money, and/or wealth to the native, while he/she's alive, and/or through his/her will. Considering children, the native may have children who may be physically, intellectually, emotionally, creatively and/or spiritually better or much better than average. Such children may achieve a lot in many spheres of their lives, and they may bring good name and many other good results to the native.

Looking at profession, such combust Moon can help the native achieve success as a fire fighter, fitness trainer, body builder, sportsman, athlete, physician, dietician, lawyer, astrologer, tantric, psychic, spiritual guru, healer, religious guru, teacher, preacher, consultant, researcher, analyst, host, artist, poet, chef, interior designer, police officer, army, air force, naval, revenue, administrative, foreign services officer, judge, doctor, scientist, engineer, politician, professional dealing in education industry, coaching, food, health, pharma, medical, nursing, homecare, real estate, agriculture, hospitality, beauty, fashion, finance, television, music, sports, media, book, publishing, fitness, travel, hotel, airline, fishing,

shipping, telecom, computer, software, IT, internet industry or some other type of professional, depending on his/her overall horoscope and running times.

Such combust Moon can help the native achieve success through a creative field as an actor, singer, musician, writer, dancer, sportsman, artist, architect, designer, developer or some other likewise professional. Taking an example, suppose combust Moon is placed in the fifth house of a horoscope in Sagittarius with benefic Sun and benefic Venus. Benefic Mercury is placed in the fourth house in Scorpio, benefic exalted Mars is placed in the sixth house in Capricorn, benefic Rahu is placed in the first house in Leo, Ketu is placed in the seventh house in Aquarius, Jupiter is placed in the third house in Libra, and retrograde Saturn is placed in the eleventh house in Gemini.

In this case, the native may become a movie director. He may possess remarkable talent, and he may come across very good amount of success, money, recognition and fame. He may deliver several hit movies, and he may receive many awards. If the finer factors and running times are supportive, he may become one of the most recognized directors of all time, and his net worth may be in multimillions.

Taking an example for a female native, suppose combust Moon is placed in the fifth house of a horoscope in Sagittarius with benefic Sun, benefic Rahu and benefic Mercury. Ketu is placed in the eleventh house in Gemini, retrograde Jupiter is placed in the twelfth house in Cancer, benefic Mars is placed in the seventh house in Aquarius, and exalted Saturn is placed in the third house in Libra. Sun and Mercury form Budhaditya Yoga in the fifth house. In this case, the native may become a singer, and she may witness good results.

If benefic Venus is placed in the third house in Libra with Saturn, the equation may become better. The native may possess remarkable singing talent, and she may come across very good amount of success, money, recognition and fame. She may deliver several hit songs, and she may receive many awards, including several Grammys. She may also write some songs. If the finer factors and running times are supportive, she may become one of the most successful singers of her time, and her net worth may be in multimillions.

On the other hand, when malefic in nature, combination of Sun and combust Moon in the fifth house of a horoscope in Sagittarius can trouble the native with problems related to father, mother, health, lifespan, love life, children, profession, finances, reputation, authority, recognition and several other problems, depending on his/her overall horoscope and running times.

Sun rules the first house, Moon rules the twelfth house, and they are placed in the fifth house. If such combination of Sun and combust Moon is influenced by malefic planets, and/or an overall malefic horoscope, the native may witness various types of problems related to or through his father, mother, children and/or lifespan. Considering parents, the native may not have a good equation with his father/mother, his parents may get divorced and he may live with his father/mother, his father/mother may suffer from a long-lasting illness, he/she may be an alcoholic and/or a drug addict, he/she may be a criminal, and/or he/she may die before native's age of 20, depending on native's overall horoscope and running times. Considering children, the native may lose one or more children through miscarriages that his wife may witness. He may witness delay in childbirth, and/or he may have children who may be physically and/or mentally troubled in some way. He may lose his children through divorce, or his children may engage in immoral/illegal activities, and he may witness bad reputation and many other problems because of them. Considering lifespan, the native may witness reduction in lifespan due to several reasons.

The native may witness delays, financial losses, setbacks, failures, job loss, bad reputation and several other problems related to or through his profession. Taking an example, suppose malefic combust Moon is placed in the fifth house of a horoscope in Sagittarius with Sun, Venus and malefic retrograde Saturn. Malefic Rahu and Jupiter form Guru Chandal Yoga in the third house in Libra, malefic Ketu forms Pitra Dosh in the ninth house in Aries, Mars is placed in the eighth house in Pisces, and Mercury is placed in the sixth house in Capricorn.

In this case, native's father as well as mother may die before his age of 15 or 10. He may not achieve much professional success till his age of 35/40, or throughout his life. He may witness financial tightness and debts, many times in his life. He may remain jobless for periods of more than 3 months, many times in his life. He may witness 2 or 3 failed marriages. He may lose one or more children to death, through miscarriages that his wife/wives may witness. He may die before his age of 60 or 55, due to drug addiction or overdose, failure of a vital organ, heart attack, or because of a fatal viral infection like COVID.

Combust Moon in Fifth House in Capricorn

When Sun and combust Moon are placed in the fifth house of a horoscope in Capricorn, Virgo rises in the ascendant. Sun rules the twelfth house, and Moon rules the eleventh house. In general, this combination is partly benefic and partly malefic here, though the benefic part is higher, in most cases. The concept of various planets exhibiting tendencies to be benefic or malefic on the basis of the houses they rule in a horoscope has been explained in the book 'Gemstones: Magic or Science?'.

Combination of Sun and combust Moon in the fifth house of horoscope in Capricorn is benefic in many cases, though it may turn malefic in some cases. It may happen when such combination is influenced by one or more malefic planets, and/or an overall malefic horoscope. The concept of a benefic planet turning malefic due to influences of malefic planets has been explained in the book 'Match Making and Manglik Dosh'.

When benefic in nature, combination of Sun and combust Moon in the fifth house of a horoscope in Capricorn can bless the native with good results related to father, mother, friends, love life, children, creativity, spiritual growth, profession, finances, reputation, authority, recognition, fame and several other good results, depending on his/her overall horoscope and running times.

Such combination of Sun and combust Moon can render various types of benefits to the native, related to or through his father, mother, children and/or friends. Considering parents, native's father/mother may be a rich man/woman, a celebrity, an officer in government or a powerful politician. The native may enjoy many benefits because of his father/mother's money, influence and/or status. He/she may give a big amount of money, and/or wealth to the native, while he/she's alive, and/or through his/her will. Considering children, the native may have children who may be physically, intellectually, emotionally, creatively and/or spiritually better or much better than average. Considering friends, some of his friends may stand by the native and they may help him get out of his problems, many times in his life.

Looking at profession, such combust Moon can help the native achieve success as a fire fighter, fitness trainer, body builder, sportsman, athlete, physician, dietician, lawyer, astrologer, tantric, psychic, spiritual guru, healer, religious guru, teacher, preacher, consultant, researcher, analyst, host, artist, poet, chef, interior designer, police officer, army, air force, naval, revenue, administrative, foreign services officer, judge, doctor, scientist, engineer, politician, professional dealing in education industry, coaching, food, health, pharma, medical, nursing, homecare, real estate, agriculture, hospitality, beauty, fashion, finance, television, music, sports, media, book, publishing, fitness, travel, hotel, airline, fishing, shipping, telecom, computer, software, IT, internet industry

or some other type of professional, depending on his/her overall horoscope and running times.

Such combust Moon can help the native achieve success through a creative field as an actor, singer, musician, writer, dancer, sportsman, artist, architect, designer, developer or some other likewise professional. Taking an example, suppose benefic combust Moon is placed in the fifth house of a horoscope in Capricorn with Sun, benefic Mercury and benefic Venus. Exalted Saturn is placed in the second house in Libra, benefic debilitated Rahu is placed in the third house in Scorpio with benefic Jupiter; and debilitated Ketu is placed in the ninth house in Taurus with Mars.

In this case, the native may become a fashion designer. He may possess remarkable talent. He may start a company which may make various types of fashion products, and he may come across very good amount of success, money, recognition and fame. He may design costumes for several celebrities, and he may receive many awards. His business may expand after his age of 35/40, and it may keep growing. If the finer factors and running times are supportive, he may become one of the most successful fashion designers of his time, and he may own a business empire worth in billions.

Taking another example, suppose benefic combust Moon is placed in the fifth house of a horoscope in Capricorn with Sun and benefic Mercury. Benefic Venus is placed in the third house in Scorpio with benefic debilitated Rahu; Saturn is placed in the ninth house in Taurus with debilitated Ketu; and benefic Jupiter is placed in the tenth house in Gemini with Mars.

In this case, the native may write fictional books. He may possess remarkable talent, and he may come across very good amount of success, money, recognition and fame. He may write in several genres including romance and drama. He may deliver several bestsellers, and he may receive many awards. If the finer factors and running times are supportive, he may become one of the most successful writers of his time, and his net worth may be in multimillions.

On the other hand, when malefic in nature, combination of Sun and combust Moon in the fifth house of a horoscope in Capricorn can trouble the native with problems related to father, mother, friends, love life, children, profession, finances, reputation, authority, recognition and several other problems, depending on his/her overall horoscope and running times.

Sun rules the twelfth house, Moon rules the eleventh house, and they are placed in the fifth house. If such combination of Sun and combust Moon is influenced by malefic planets, and/or an overall malefic horoscope, the native may witness various types of problems related to or through his father, mother, children and/or friends. Considering parents, the native may not have a good equation with his father/mother, his parents may get divorced and he may live with his father/mother, his father/mother may suffer from a long-lasting illness, he/she may be an alcoholic and/or a drug addict, he/she may be a criminal, and/or he/she may die before native's age of 20, depending on native's overall horoscope and running times. Considering children, the native may lose one or more children through miscarriages that his wife may witness. He may witness delay in childbirth, and/or he may have children who may be physically and/ or mentally troubled in some way. He may lose his children through divorce, or his children may engage in immoral/ illegal activities, and he may witness bad reputation and many other problems because of them. Considering friends, some of his friends may be selfish, opportunists, criminal-minded, criminals, drug addicts, traitors and/or they may have some other negative traits. The native may witness several problems because of such friends, many times in his life. In an extreme case, one or more of his good friends may die before native's age of 40 or 35.

The native may witness delays, financial losses, setbacks, failures, job loss, bad reputation and several other problems related to or through his profession. Taking an example, suppose combust Moon is placed in the fifth house of a horoscope in Capricorn with Venus, malefic Sun and malefic exalted Mars. Benefic Mercury is placed in the fourth house in Sagittarius with Saturn; malefic debilitated Rahu is placed in the seventh house in Pisces, malefic debilitated Ketu is placed in the first house in Virgo, and retrograde Jupiter is placed in the sixth house in Aquarius.

In this case, native's father may die before native's age of 10 or 5. The native may have a difficult equation with his mother, and he may witness a troublesome childhood. He may not achieve much professional success till his age of 35/40, or throughout his life, though he may earn well at times. He may witness financial losses and bad reputation through profession. He may lose one or more good friends to death, before his age of 35/30. He may witness 1 or 2 failed marriages. He may lose his first wife to death. He may lose one or more children to death, through miscarriages that his wife/wives may witness.

Combust Moon in Fifth House in Aquarius

When Sun and combust Moon are placed in the fifth house of a horoscope in Aquarius, Libra rises in the ascendant. Sun rules the eleventh house, and Moon rules the tenth house. In general, this combination is benefic here, in most cases. The concept of various planets exhibiting tendencies to be benefic or malefic on the basis of the houses they rule in a horoscope has been explained in the book 'Gemstones: Magic or Science?'.

Combination of Sun and combust Moon in the fifth house of horoscope in Aquarius is benefic in most cases, though it may turn malefic in some cases. It may happen when such combination is influenced by one or more malefic planets, and/or an overall malefic horoscope. The concept of a benefic planet turning malefic due to influences of malefic planets has been explained in the book 'Match Making and Manglik Dosh'.

When benefic in nature, combination of Sun and combust Moon in the fifth house of a horoscope in Aquarius can bless the native with good results related to father, mother, friends, love life, children, creativity, spiritual growth, profession, finances, reputation, authority, recognition, fame and several other good results, depending on his/her overall horoscope and running times.

Such combination of Sun and combust Moon can render various types of benefits to the native, related to or through his father, mother, children and/or friends. Considering parents, native's father/mother may be a rich man/ woman, a celebrity, an officer in government or a powerful politician. The native may enjoy many benefits because of his father/mother's money, influence and/or status. He/ she may give a big amount of money, and/or wealth to the native, while he/she's alive, and/or through his/her will. Considering children, the native may have children who may be physically, intellectually, emotionally, creatively and/or spiritually better or much better than average. Such children may achieve a lot in many spheres of their lives, and they may bring good name and many other good results to the native. Considering friends, some of his friends may stand by the native and they may help him get out of his problems, many times in his life.

Looking at profession, such combust Moon can help the native achieve success as a fire fighter, fitness trainer, body builder, sportsman, athlete, physician, dietician, lawyer, astrologer, tantric, psychic, spiritual guru, healer, religious guru, teacher, preacher, consultant, researcher, analyst, host, artist, poet, chef, interior designer, police officer, army, air force, naval, revenue, administrative, foreign services officer, judge, doctor, scientist, engineer, politician, professional dealing in education industry, coaching, food, health, pharma, medical, nursing, homecare, real estate, agriculture, hospitality, beauty, fashion, finance, television, music, sports, media, book, publishing, fitness, travel, hotel, airline, fishing, shipping, telecom, computer, software, IT, internet industry or some other type of professional, depending on his/her overall horoscope and running times.

Taking an example, suppose benefic combust Moon is placed in the fifth house of a horoscope in Aquarius with Venus and benefic Sun. Mercury is placed in the fourth house in Capricorn, benefic Mars is placed in the third house in Sagittarius with Jupiter; benefic exalted Rahu is placed in the twelfth house in Virgo, exalted Ketu is placed in the sixth house in Pisces, and benefic Saturn is placed in the eighth house in Taurus.

In this case, the native may start a company which may make video games, and he may come across very good amount of success, money and recognition. His business may expand after his age of 35/40, and it may keep growing. If the finer factors and running times are supportive, he may own a business empire worth in billions, by his age of 55/60.

Such combust Moon can help the native achieve success through a creative field as an actor, singer, musician, writer, dancer, sportsman, artist, architect, designer, developer or some other likewise professional. Taking an example, suppose benefic combust Moon is placed in the fifth house of a horoscope in Aquarius with Venus, benefic Sun and benefic Rahu. Benefic Mars is placed in the eleventh house in Leo with Ketu; benefic retrograde Saturn is placed in the third house in Sagittarius, Mercury is placed in the fourth house in Capricorn, and retrograde Jupiter is placed in the second house in Scorpio.

In this case, the native may become an actor. He may possess remarkable acting talent, and he may come across very good amount of success, money, recognition and fame. He may perform very well in the genres of action, drama and romance. He may deliver several hit movies, and he may receive many awards. If the finer factors and running times are supportive, he may become one of the most successful actors of his time, and his net worth may be in multimillions.

On the other hand, when malefic in nature, combination of Sun and combust Moon in the fifth house of a horoscope in Aquarius can trouble the native with problems related to father, mother, friends, love life, children, profession, finances, reputation, authority, recognition and several other problems, depending on his/her overall horoscope and running times.

Sun rules the eleventh house, Moon rules the tenth house, and they are placed in the fifth house. If such combination of Sun and combust Moon is influenced by malefic planets, and/or an overall malefic horoscope, the native may witness various types of problems related to or through his father, mother, children and/or friends. Considering parents, the native may not have a good equation with his father/mother, his parents may get divorced and he may live with his father/mother, his father/mother may suffer from a long-lasting illness, he/she may be an alcoholic and/or a drug addict, he/she may be a criminal, and/or he/she may die before native's age of 20, depending on native's overall horoscope and running times. Considering children, the native may lose one or more children through miscarriages that his wife may witness. He may witness delay in childbirth, and/or he may have children who may be physically and/or mentally troubled in some way. He may lose his children through divorce, or his children may engage in immoral/illegal activities, and he may witness bad reputation and many other problems because of them. Considering friends, some of his friends may be selfish, opportunists, criminal-minded, criminals, drug addicts, traitors and/or they may have some other negative traits. The native may witness several problems because of such friends, many times in his life. In an extreme case, one or more of his good friends may die before native's age of 40 or 35.

The native may witness delays, financial losses, setbacks, failures, job loss, bad reputation and several other problems related to or through his profession. Taking an example, suppose combust Moon is placed in the fifth house of a horoscope in Aquarius with Sun, Venus, Mercury and malefic Ketu. Malefic Rahu is placed in the eleventh house in Leo, malefic Jupiter is placed in the sixth house in Pisces with Mars; and Saturn is placed in the eighth house in Taurus. Grahan Yoga is formed in the fifth house.

In this case, native's father as well as mother may die before his age of 20 or 15. He may not find a permanent profession till his age of 35/40, or throughout his life, though he may earn well at times. He may witness financial losses and bad reputation through profession. He may witness several problems because of some of his friends, including financial losses and betrayals. He may witness 1 or 2 failed marriages. He may lose one of more children to death, through miscarriages that his wife/wives may witness.

Combust Moon in Fifth House in Pisces

When Sun and combust Moon are placed in the fifth house of a horoscope in Pisces, Scorpio rises in the ascendant. Sun rules the tenth house, and Moon rules the ninth house. In general, this combination is benefic here, in most cases. The concept of various planets exhibiting tendencies to be benefic or malefic on the basis of the houses they rule in a horoscope has been explained in the book 'Gemstones: Magic or Science?'.

Combination of Sun and combust Moon in the fifth house of horoscope in Pisces is benefic in most cases, though it may turn malefic in some cases. It may happen when such combination is influenced by one or more malefic planets, and/or an overall malefic horoscope. The concept of a benefic planet turning malefic due to influences of malefic planets has been explained in the book 'Match Making and Manglik Dosh'.

When benefic in nature, combination of Sun and combust Moon in the fifth house of a horoscope in Pisces can bless the native with good results related to father, mother, love life, children, creativity, spiritual growth, profession, finances, reputation, authority, recognition, fame and several other good results, depending on his/her overall horoscope and running times.

Such combination of Sun and combust Moon can render various types of benefits to the native, related to or through his father, mother and/or children. Considering parents, native's father/mother may be a rich man/woman, a celebrity, an officer in government or a powerful politician. The native may enjoy many benefits because of his father/mother's money, influence and/or status. He/she may give a big amount of money, and/or wealth to the native, while he/she's alive, and/or through his/her will. Considering children, the native may have children who may be physically, intellectually, emotionally, creatively and/or spiritually better or much better than average. Such children may achieve a lot in many spheres of their lives, and they may bring good name and many other good results to the native.

Looking at profession, such combust Moon can help the native achieve success as a fire fighter, fitness trainer, body builder, sportsman, athlete, physician, dietician, lawyer, astrologer, tantric, psychic, spiritual guru, healer, religious guru, teacher, preacher, consultant, researcher, analyst, host, artist, poet, chef, interior designer, police officer, army, air force, naval, revenue, administrative, foreign services officer, judge, doctor, scientist, engineer, politician, professional dealing in education industry, coaching, food, health, pharma, medical, nursing, homecare, real estate, agriculture, hospitality, beauty, fashion, finance, television, music, sports, media, book, publishing, fitness, travel, hotel, airline, fishing, shipping, telecom, computer, software, IT, internet industry

or some other type of professional, depending on his/her overall horoscope and running times.

Such combust Moon can help the native achieve success through a creative field as an actor, singer, musician, writer, dancer, sportsman, artist, architect, designer, developer or some other likewise professional. Taking an example, suppose benefic combust Moon is placed in the fifth house of a horoscope in Pisces with benefic Sun. Mercury is placed in the sixth house in Aries, Mars is placed in the second house in Sagittarius, benefic Rahu is placed in the tenth house in Leo, Ketu is placed in the fourth house in Aquarius, Venus is placed in the seventh house in Taurus, and benefic retrograde Saturn is placed in the twelfth house in Libra. In this case, the native may become an actor, and he may witness good results.

If benefic Jupiter is placed in the first house in Scorpio, the equation may become better. The native may possess remarkable acting talent, and he may come across very good amount of success, money, recognition and fame. He may perform very well in the genres of action, drama and romance. He may deliver several hit movies, and he may receive many awards, including more than one Oscar. If the finer factors and running times are supportive, he may become one of the greatest actors of all time, and his net worth may be in billions.

Taking another example, suppose benefic combust Moon is placed in the fifth house of a horoscope in Pisces with Mars, retrograde Mercury and benefic Sun. Benefic Rahu is placed in the fourth house in Aquarius with Venus; Ketu is placed in the tenth house in Leo, benefic retrograde Jupiter is placed in the twelfth house in Libra, and benefic retrograde Saturn is placed in the second house in Sagittarius.

In this case, the native may write fictional as well as non-fictional books. He may possess remarkable talent, and he may come across very good amount of success, money, recognition and fame. He may write in several genres, including drama, romance and philosophy. He may deliver several bestsellers, and he may receive many awards. If the finer factors and running times are supportive, he may become one of the most successful writers of his time, and his net worth may be in multimillions.

On the other hand, when malefic in nature, combination of Sun and combust Moon in the fifth house of a horoscope in Pisces can trouble the native with problems related to father, mother, love life, children, profession, finances, reputation, authority, recognition and several other problems, depending on his/her overall horoscope and running times.

Sun rules the tenth house, Moon rules the ninth house, and they are placed in the fifth house. If such combination of Sun and combust Moon is influenced by malefic planets, and/or an overall malefic horoscope, the native may witness various types of problems related to or through his father, mother and/or children. Considering parents, the native may not have a good equation with his father/mother, his parents may get divorced and he may live with his father/ mother, his father/mother may suffer from a long-lasting illness, he/she may be an alcoholic and/or a drug addict, he/she may be a criminal, and/or he/she may die before native's age of 20, depending on native's overall horoscope and running times. Considering children, the native may lose one or more children through miscarriages that his wife may witness. He may witness delay in childbirth, and/or he may have children who may be physically and/or mentally troubled in some way. He may lose his children through divorce, or his children may engage in immoral/illegal activities, and he may witness bad reputation and many other problems because of them.

The native may witness delays, financial losses, setbacks, failures, job loss, bad reputation and several other problems related to or through his profession. Taking an example, suppose combust Moon is placed in the fifth house of a horoscope in Pisces with Sun, Mars, malefic retrograde Mercury and malefic debilitated Rahu. Malefic debilitated Ketu is placed in the eleventh house in Virgo, malefic Venus is placed in the seventh house in Taurus with Saturn; and benefic Jupiter is placed in the fourth house in Aquarius. Grahan Yoga is formed in the fifth house.

In this case, native's father may die before his age of 10 or 5. His mother may get married again, but the native may not have a good equation with his stepfather. His stepfather may also die before native's age of 20 or 15. The native may not find a permanent profession till his age of 35/40, or throughout his life, though he may earn well at times. He may remain jobless for periods of more than 3 months, many times in his life. He may not get married till his age of 35/40, or throughout his life. He may not have a child till his age of 40/45, or throughout his life.

Combust Moon in Sixth House in Aries

When Sun and combust Moon are placed in the sixth house of a horoscope in Aries, Scorpio rises in the ascendant. Sun rules the tenth house, and Moon rules the ninth house. In general, this combination is benefic here, in many cases. The concept of various planets exhibiting tendencies to be benefic or malefic on the basis of the houses they rule in a horoscope has been explained in the book 'Gemstones: Magic or Science?'.

Combination of Sun and combust Moon in the sixth house of horoscope in Aries is benefic in many cases, though it may turn malefic in some cases. It may happen when such combination is influenced by one or more malefic planets, and/or an overall malefic horoscope. The concept of a benefic planet turning malefic due to influences of malefic planets has been explained in the book 'Match Making and Manglik Dosh'.

When benefic in nature, combination of Sun and combust Moon in the sixth house of a horoscope in Aries can bless the native with good results related to father, mother, profession, finances, reputation, authority, recognition, fame and several other good results, depending on his/her overall horoscope and running times.

Such combination of Sun and combust Moon can render various types of benefits to the native, related to or through his father and/or mother. Considering parents, native's father/mother may be a rich man/woman, a celebrity, an officer in government or a powerful politician. The native may enjoy many benefits because of his father/mother's money, influence and/or status. He/she may give a big amount of money, and/or wealth to the native, while he/she's alive, and/or through his/her will.

Looking at profession, such combust Moon can help the native achieve success as a fire fighter, fitness trainer, body builder, sportsman, athlete, physician, dietician, lawyer, astrologer, tantric, psychic, spiritual guru, healer, religious guru, teacher, preacher, consultant, actor, singer, musician, writer, dancer, sportsman, artist, architect, designer, developer, poet, chef, interior designer, host, researcher, analyst, professional dealing in education industry, coaching, food, health, pharma, medical, nursing, homecare, real estate, agriculture, hospitality, beauty, fashion, finance, television, music, sports, media, book, publishing, fitness, travel, hotel, airline, fishing, shipping, telecom, computer, software, IT, internet industry or some other type of professional, depending on his/her overall horoscope and running times.

Taking an example, suppose benefic combust Moon is placed in the sixth house of a horoscope in Aries with Mercury and benefic exalted Sun. Benefic Saturn is placed in the eighth house in Gemini with Venus; benefic Moon is placed in the fourth house in Aquarius, benefic debilitated

Rahu is placed in the first house in Scorpio, and debilitated Ketu is placed in the seventh house in Taurus. In this case, the native may become a doctor, and he may witness good results.

If benefic exalted Jupiter is placed in the ninth house in Cancer, the equation may become better. The native may specialize in cardiology. He may possess remarkable knowledge of his field, and he may come across very good amount of success, money and recognition. He may have a high success rate, and he may write some books on various topics. If the finer factors and running times are supportive, he may become one of the most successful cardiologists of his region, and his net worth may be in multimillions.

Such combust Moon can bless the native with authority in government as a police officer, army, air force, naval, revenue, administrative, foreign services officer, judge, doctor, scientist, engineer, politician or some other type of professional. Taking an example, suppose benefic combust Moon is placed in the sixth house of a horoscope in Aries with retrograde Mercury and benefic exalted Sun. Mars is placed in the tenth house in Leo, benefic debilitated Rahu is placed in the first house in Scorpio, debilitated Ketu is placed in the seventh house in Taurus with Venus; and benefic Moon is placed in the third house in Capricorn. In this case, the native may become an officer in police force, and he may enjoy a good career.

If benefic Saturn forms Shasha Yoga in the fourth house in Aquarius, the equation may become better. In this case, the native may achieve success in civil exams, and he may get selected for the highest possible direct rank in police force. He may serve at several important posts during his career, and he may come across very good amount of success, recognition and authority. If the finer factors and running times are supportive, he may serve as chief of police of a state, before retirement.

On the other hand, when malefic in nature, combination of Sun and combust Moon in the sixth house of a horoscope in Aries can trouble the native with problems related to father, mother, profession, finances, reputation, authority, recognition and several other problems, depending on his/ her overall horoscope and running times.

Sun rules the tenth house, Moon rules the ninth house, and they are placed in the sixth house. If such combination of Sun and combust Moon is influenced by malefic planets, and/or an overall malefic horoscope, the native may witness various types of problems related to or through his father and/or mother. Considering parents, the native may not have a good equation with his father/mother, his parents may get divorced and he may live with his father/ mother, his father/mother may suffer from a long-lasting illness, he/she may be an alcoholic and/or a drug addict, he/she may be a criminal, and/or he/she may die before native's age of 20, depending on native's overall horoscope and running times. The native may not know his biological father/mother, or his father/mother may refuse to accept him as his/her son, as native may be born from a secret love affair of his father/mother, and he/she may give him to someone else or to an orphanage. In an extreme case, the native may kill his father/mother for some reason, or his father/mother may kill him, depending on native's overall horoscope and running times.

The native may witness delays, financial losses, setbacks, failures, job loss, bad reputation and several other problems related to or through his profession. Taking an example, suppose combust Moon is placed in the sixth house of a horoscope in Aries with exalted Sun, malefic Mercury and malefic Venus. Malefic Ketu is placed in the fourth house in Aquarius with Mars; malefic Rahu is placed in the tenth house in Leo, Saturn is placed in the eighth house in Gemini, and Jupiter is placed in the twelfth house in Libra.

In this case, native's father as well as mother may die before his age of 15 or 10. He may not find a permanent profession throughout his life, and he may only find temporary jobs. He may remain jobless for periods of more than 3 months, many times in his life. He may witness financial tightness and debts, many times in his life. He may witness 1 or 2 failed marriages.

Combust Moon in Sixth House in Taurus

When Sun and combust Moon are placed in the sixth house of a horoscope in Taurus, Sagittarius rises in the ascendant. Sun rules the ninth house, and Moon rules the eighth house. In general, this combination is partly benefic and partly malefic here, though the malefic part is higher, in most cases. The concept of various planets exhibiting tendencies to be benefic or malefic on the basis of the houses they rule in a horoscope has been explained in the book 'Gemstones: Magic or Science?'.

Combination of Sun and combust Moon in the sixth house of horoscope in Taurus is malefic in many cases, though it may turn benefic in some cases. It may happen when such combination is influenced by one or more benefic planets, and/or an overall benefic horoscope. The concept of a malefic planet turning benefic due to influences of benefic planets has been explained in the book 'Match Making and Manglik Dosh'.

When benefic in nature, combination of Sun and combust Moon in the sixth house of a horoscope in Taurus can bless the native with good results related to father, mother, lifespan, profession, finances, reputation, authority, recognition, fame and several other good results, depending on his/her overall horoscope and running times.

Such combination of Sun and combust Moon can render various types of benefits to the native, related to or through his father and/or mother. Considering parents, native's father/mother may be a rich man/woman, a celebrity, an officer in government or a powerful politician. The native may enjoy many benefits because of his father/mother's money, influence and/or status. He/she may give a big amount of money, and/or wealth to the native, while he/she's alive, and/or through his/her will.

Looking at profession, such combust Moon can help the native achieve success as a fire fighter, fitness trainer, body builder, sportsman, athlete, physician, dietician, lawyer, astrologer, tantric, psychic, spiritual guru, healer, religious guru, teacher, preacher, consultant, actor, singer, musician, writer, dancer, sportsman, artist, architect, designer, developer, poet, chef, interior designer, host, researcher, analyst, professional dealing in education industry, coaching, food, health, pharma, medical, nursing, homecare, real estate, agriculture, hospitality, beauty, fashion, finance, television, music, sports, media, book, publishing, fitness, travel, hotel, airline, fishing, shipping, telecom, computer, software, IT, internet industry or some other type of professional, depending on his/her overall horoscope and running times.

Taking an example, suppose combust Moon is placed in the sixth house of a horoscope in Taurus with benefic Sun. Benefic Mercury is placed in the seventh house in Gemini with Venus; benefic retrograde Jupiter forms Hamsa Yoga in the first house in Sagittarius, benefic retrograde Saturn is placed in the eighth house in Cancer, Mars is placed in the ninth house in Leo, benefic Rahu is placed in the eleventh house in Libra, and Ketu is placed in the fifth house in Aries. Mercury forms Bhadra Yoga in the seventh house.

In this case, the native may start an airline, and he may come across very good amount of success, money and recognition. His business may expand after his age of 35/40, and it may keep growing. He may also invest in hotel industry, and he may witness profits. If the finer factors and running times are supportive, he may own a business empire worth in billions, by his age of 55/60.

Such combust Moon can bless the native with authority in government as a police officer, army, air force, naval, revenue, administrative, foreign services officer, judge, doctor, scientist, engineer, politician or some other type of professional. Taking an example, suppose combust Moon is placed in the sixth house of a horoscope in Taurus with Venus, benefic Sun and benefic retrograde Mercury. Benefic Rahu is placed in the first house in Sagittarius with Mars; Ketu is placed in the seventh house in Gemini, and benefic Saturn is placed in the eighth house in Cancer. Sun and Mercury form Budhaditya Yoga in the sixth house. In this case, the native may become an officer in army, and he may enjoy a good career.

If benefic retrograde Jupiter is placed in the ninth house in Leo, the equation may become better. In this case, the native may achieve success in competitive exams, and he may get selected for the highest possible direct rank in army. He may serve at several important posts during his career, and he may come across very good amount of success, recognition and authority. If the finer factors and running times are supportive, he may serve at one of the top 2 ranks in army, before retirement.

On the other hand, when malefic in nature, combination of Sun and combust Moon in the sixth house of a horoscope in Taurus can trouble the native with problems related to father, mother, lifespan, profession, finances, reputation, authority, recognition and several other problems, depending on his/her overall horoscope and running times.

Sun rules the ninth house, Moon rules the eighth house, and they are placed in the sixth house. If such combination of Sun and combust Moon is influenced by malefic planets, and/or an overall malefic horoscope, the native may witness various types of problems related to or through his father, mother and/or lifespan. Considering parents, the native may not have a good equation with his father/mother, his parents may get divorced and he may live with his father/mother, his father/mother may suffer from a long-lasting illness, he/she may be an alcoholic and/or a drug addict, he/she may be a criminal, and/or he/she may die before native's age of 20, depending on native's overall horoscope and running times. The native may not know his biological father/mother, or his father/mother may refuse to accept him as his/her son, as native may be born from a secret love affair of his father/mother, and he/she may give him to someone else or to an orphanage. In an extreme case, the native may kill his father/mother for some reason, or his father/mother may kill him, depending on native's overall horoscope and running times. Considering lifespan, the native may witness reduction in lifespan due to several reasons. For example, the native may die in an accident, through a natural disaster, due to a fatal disease, due to a fatal viral infection like COVID, due to drug addiction, he may commit suicide, or someone may kill him intentionally or unintentionally.

The native may witness delays, financial losses, setbacks, failures, job loss, bad reputation and several other problems related to or through his profession. Taking an example, suppose malefic combust Moon is placed in the sixth house of a horoscope in Taurus with Sun, Mercury and Mars. Malefic Venus is placed in the seventh house in Gemini, malefic Rahu forms Pitra Dosh in ninth house in Leo, malefic Ketu is placed in the third house in Aquarius with retrograde Jupiter; and Saturn is placed in the twelfth house in Scorpio. Guru Chandal Yoga is formed in the third house.

In this case, native's father may die before native's age of 15 or 10. His mother may get married again, but he may not have a good equation with his stepfather. The native may not find a permanent profession throughout his life, and he may keep losing jobs, though he may earn well at times. He may not remain jobless for periods of more than 3 months, many times in his life. He may witness 1 or 2 failed marriages. He may die before his age of 60 or 55, due to a heart attack, in an accident, or because of a fatal viral infection like COVID.

Combust Moon in Sixth House in Gemini

When Sun and combust Moon are placed in the sixth house of a horoscope in Gemini, Capricorn rises in the ascendant. Sun rules the eighth house, and Moon rules the seventh house. In general, this combination is partly benefic and partly malefic here, though the malefic part is higher, in most cases. The concept of various planets exhibiting tendencies to be benefic or malefic on the basis of the houses they rule in a horoscope has been explained in the book 'Gemstones: Magic or Science?'.

Combination of Sun and combust Moon in the sixth house of horoscope in Gemini is malefic in many cases, though it may turn benefic in some cases. It may happen when such combination is influenced by one or more benefic planets, and/or an overall benefic horoscope. The concept of a malefic planet turning benefic due to influences of benefic planets has been explained in the book 'Match Making and Manglik Dosh'.

When benefic in nature, combination of Sun and combust Moon in the sixth house of a horoscope in Gemini can bless the native with good results related to father, mother, marriage, husband, wife, lifespan, profession, finances, reputation, authority, recognition, fame and several other good results, depending on his/her overall horoscope and running times.

Such combination of Sun and combust Moon can render various types of benefits to the native, related to or through his father, mother and/or marriage. Considering parents, native's father/mother may be a rich man/woman, a celebrity, an officer in government or a powerful politician. The native may enjoy many benefits because of his father/mother's money, influence and/or status. He/she may give a big amount of money, and/or wealth to the native, while he/she's alive, and/or through his/her will. Considering marriage, the native may get married to a woman who may be beautiful, rich, a celebrity, an officer in government, a powerful politician, a successful businesswoman, and/or a citizen of a foreign country. The native may witness several benefits due to or through his wife and/or her family members.

Looking at profession, such combust Moon can help the native achieve success as a fire fighter, fitness trainer, body builder, sportsman, athlete, physician, dietician, lawyer, astrologer, tantric, psychic, spiritual guru, healer, religious guru, teacher, preacher, consultant, researcher, analyst, host, artist, poet, chef, interior designer, professional dealing in education industry, coaching, food, health, pharma, medical, nursing, homecare, real estate, agriculture, hospitality, beauty, fashion, finance, television, music, sports, media, book, publishing, fitness, travel, hotel, airline, fishing, shipping, telecom, computer, software, IT, internet industry or some other type of professional, depending on his/her overall horoscope and running times.

Such combust Moon can help the native achieve success through a creative field as an actor, singer, musician, writer, dancer, sportsman, artist, architect, designer, developer or some other likewise professional. Taking an example, suppose benefic combust Moon is placed in the sixth house of a horoscope in Gemini with Sun and benefic Rahu. Ketu is placed in the twelfth house in Sagittarius, benefic Venus is placed in the fifth house in Taurus with Mercury; Jupiter is placed in the third house in Pisces, benefic Mars is placed in the ninth house in Virgo, and benefic retrograde Saturn is placed in the eleventh house in Scorpio.

In this case, the native may write fictional books. He may possess remarkable writing talent, and he may come across very good amount of success, money, recognition and fame. He may write in several genres, including drama, romance and mystery. He may deliver several bestsellers, and he may receive many awards. If the finer factors and running times are supportive, he may become one of the most successful writers of his time, and his net worth may be in multimillions.

Such combust Moon can bless the native with authority in government as a police officer, army, air force, naval, revenue, administrative, foreign services officer, judge, doctor, scientist, engineer, politician or some other type of professional. Taking an example, suppose benefic combust Moon is placed in the sixth house of a horoscope in Gemini with Sun. Benefic Venus is placed in the seventh house in Cancer with retrograde Mercury and benefic Saturn; benefic Mars is placed in the ninth house in Virgo, benefic Rahu is placed in the tenth house in Libra, Ketu is placed in the fourth house in Aries, and retrograde Jupiter is placed in the first house in Capricorn.

In this case, the native may engage in politics, and he may come across very good amount of success, recognition, authority and fame. He may win several elections, and he may become chief minister or governor of a state. If the finer factors and running times are supportive, he may serve at one such post, more than once.

On the other hand, when malefic in nature, combination of Sun and combust Moon in the sixth house of a horoscope in Gemini can trouble the native with problems related to father, mother, marriage, husband, wife, lifespan, profession, finances, reputation, authority, recognition and several other problems, depending on his/her overall horoscope and running times.

Sun rules the eighth house, Moon rules the seventh house, and they are placed in the sixth house. If such combination of Sun and combust Moon is influenced by malefic planets, and/or an overall malefic horoscope, the native may witness various types of problems related to or through his father, mother, marriage and/or lifespan. Considering parents, the native may not have a good equation with his father/mother, his parents may get divorced and he may live with his father/mother, his father/mother may suffer from a long-lasting illness, he/she may be an alcoholic and/or a drug addict, he/she may be a criminal, and/or he/she may die before native's age of 20, depending on native's overall horoscope and running times. Considering marriage, the native may witness delay/disturbances in marriage, and/or one or more failed marriages. He may have serious differences of opinion with his wife, she may suffer from a long-lasting illness, she may be an alcoholic and/or a drug addict, she may be a criminal, she may not be loyal to him, she may have extramarital affair/affairs, and/or she may die within 10 or 5 years of marriage.

Considering lifespan, the native may witness reduction in lifespan due to several reasons.

The native may witness delays, financial losses, setbacks, failures, job loss, bad reputation and several other problems related to or through his profession. Taking an example, suppose combust Moon is placed in the sixth house of a horoscope in Gemini with Venus, malefic Jupiter and malefic Sun. Retrograde Mercury is placed in the seventh house in Cancer, Mars is placed in the eighth house in Leo, malefic Ketu is placed in the tenth house in Libra with exalted Saturn; and malefic Rahu is placed in the fourth house in Aries.

In this case, native's mother may die before his age of 10 or 5. His father may get married again, but the native may not have a good equation with his stepmother. He may not achieve much professional success till his age of 35/40, or throughout his life, though he may earn well at times. He may remain jobless for periods of more than 6 months, many times in his life. He may witness 1 or 2 failed marriages. He may lose his first wife to death. He may die before his age of 60 or 55, due to a heart attack, in an accident, because of a fatal viral infection like COVID, someone may kill him, or he may commit suicide.

Combust Moon in Sixth House in Cancer

When Sun and combust Moon are placed in the sixth house of a horoscope in Cancer, Aquarius rises in the ascendant. Sun rules the seventh house, and Moon rules the sixth house. In general, this combination is partly benefic and partly malefic here, though the malefic part is higher, in most cases. The concept of various planets exhibiting tendencies to be benefic or malefic on the basis of the houses they rule in a horoscope has been explained in the book 'Gemstones: Magic or Science?'.

Combination of Sun and combust Moon in the sixth house of horoscope in Cancer is malefic in many cases, though it may turn benefic in some cases. It may happen when such combination is influenced by one or more benefic planets, and/or an overall benefic horoscope. The concept of a malefic planet turning benefic due to influences of benefic planets has been explained in the book 'Match Making and Manglik Dosh'.

When benefic in nature, combination of Sun and combust Moon in the sixth house of a horoscope in Cancer can bless the native with good results related to father, mother, marriage, husband, wife, profession, finances, reputation, authority, recognition, fame and several other good results, depending on his/her overall horoscope and running times.

Such combination of Sun and combust Moon can render various types of benefits to the native, related to or through his father, mother and/or marriage. Considering parents, native's father/mother may be a rich man/woman, a celebrity, an officer in government or a powerful politician. The native may enjoy many benefits because of his father/mother's money, influence and/or status. He/she may give a big amount of money, and/or wealth to the native, while he/she's alive, and/or through his/her will. Considering marriage, the native may get married to a woman who may be beautiful, rich, a celebrity, an officer in government, a powerful politician, a successful businesswoman, and/or a citizen of a foreign country. The native may witness several benefits due to or through his wife and/or her family members.

Looking at profession, such combust Moon can help the native achieve success as a fire fighter, fitness trainer, body builder, sportsman, athlete, physician, dietician, lawyer, astrologer, tantric, psychic, spiritual guru, healer, religious guru, teacher, preacher, consultant, actor, singer, musician, writer, dancer, sportsman, artist, architect, designer, developer, poet, chef, interior designer, host, researcher, analyst, professional dealing in education industry, coaching, food, health, pharma, medical, nursing, homecare, real estate, agriculture, hospitality, beauty, fashion, finance, television, music, sports, media, book, publishing, fitness, travel, hotel, airline, fishing, shipping, telecom, computer, software, IT, internet industry or some other type of professional, depending on his/her overall horoscope and running times.

Taking an example, suppose combust Moon is placed in the sixth house of a horoscope in Cancer with benefic Sun. Benefic Venus is placed in the seventh house in Leo, exalted Saturn is placed in the ninth house in Libra, benefic Mars is placed in the eleventh house in Sagittarius with benefic Rahu; and benefic Jupiter is placed in the fifth house in Gemini with Mercury and Ketu.

In this case, the native may start a company which may handle financial investment portfolios of various clients, and he may come across very good amount of success, money and recognition. His company may invest in stocks, funds and other options, to get profit for clients. His business may expand after his age of 35/40, and it may keep growing. If the finer factors and running times are supportive, he may own a business empire worth in billions, by his age of 55/60.

Such combust Moon can bless the native with authority in government as a police officer, army, air force, naval, revenue, administrative, foreign services officer, judge, doctor, scientist, engineer, politician or some other type of professional. Taking an example, suppose combust Moon is placed in the sixth house of a horoscope in Cancer with benefic Sun. Benefic Venus is placed in the seventh house in Leo with retrograde Mercury and benefic Rahu; benefic retrograde Jupiter is placed in the first house in Aquarius with Ketu; and benefic Mars is placed in the ninth house in Libra with exalted Saturn.

In this case, the native may achieve success in civil exams, and he may get selected for the highest possible direct rank in administrative services. He may serve at several important posts during his career, and he may come across very good amount of success, recognition and authority. If the finer factors and running times are supportive, he may serve as the head of an administrative department, before retirement.

On the other hand, when malefic in nature, combination of Sun and combust Moon in the sixth house of a horoscope in Cancer can trouble the native with problems related to father, mother, marriage, husband, wife, profession, finances, reputation, authority, recognition and several other problems, depending on his/her overall horoscope and running times.

Sun rules the seventh house, Moon rules the sixth house, and they are placed in the sixth house. If such combination of Sun and combust Moon is influenced by malefic planets, and/or an overall malefic horoscope, the native may witness various types of problems related to or through his father, mother and/or marriage. Considering parents, the native may not have a good equation with his father/mother, his parents may get divorced and he may live with his father/mother, his father/mother may suffer from a long-lasting illness, he/she may be an alcoholic and/or a drug addict, he/she may be a criminal, and/or he/she may die before native's age of 20, depending on native's overall horoscope and running times. The native may not know his biological father/mother, or his father/mother may refuse to accept him as his/her son, as native may be born from a secret love affair of his father/mother, and he/she may give him to someone else or to an orphanage. Considering marriage, the native may witness delay/disturbances in marriage, and/or one or more failed marriages. He may have serious differences of opinion with his wife, she may suffer from a long-lasting illness, she may be an alcoholic and/or a drug addict, she may be a criminal, she may not be loyal to him, she may have extramarital affair/affairs, and/or she may die within 10 or 5 years of marriage.

The native may witness delays, financial losses, setbacks, failures, job loss, bad reputation and several other problems related to or through his profession. Taking an example, suppose malefic combust Moon is placed in the sixth house of a horoscope in Cancer with Sun, retrograde Mercury and malefic Ketu. Malefic Rahu is placed in the twelfth house in Capricorn with debilitated Jupiter; debilitated Venus is placed in the eighth house in Virgo, benefic Mars is placed in the seventh house in Leo, and Saturn is placed in the second house in Pisces. Grahan Yoga is formed in the sixth house whereas Guru Chandal Yoga is formed in the twelfth house.

In this case, native's mother may die before his age of 10/5, and his father may die before native's age of 20/15. The native may not achieve much professional success till his age of 35/40, or throughout his life, though he may earn well at times. He may remain jobless for periods of more than 3 months, many times in his life. He may witness 1 or 2 failed marriages.

Combust Moon in Sixth House in Leo

When Sun and combust Moon are placed in the sixth house of a horoscope in Leo, Pisces rises in the ascendant. Sun rules the sixth house, and Moon rules the fifth house. In general, this combination is partly benefic and partly malefic here, though the malefic part is higher, in most cases. The concept of various planets exhibiting tendencies to be benefic or malefic on the basis of the houses they rule in a horoscope has been explained in the book 'Gemstones: Magic or Science?'.

Combination of Sun and combust Moon in the sixth house of horoscope in Leo is malefic in many cases, though it may turn benefic in some cases. It may happen when such combination is influenced by one or more benefic planets, and/or an overall benefic horoscope. The concept of a malefic planet turning benefic due to influences of benefic planets has been explained in the book 'Match Making and Manglik Dosh'.

When benefic in nature, combination of Sun and combust Moon in the sixth house of a horoscope in Leo can bless the native with good results related to father, mother, love life, children, creativity, profession, finances, reputation, authority, recognition, fame and several other good results, depending on his/her overall horoscope and running times.

Such combination of Sun and combust Moon can render various types of benefits to the native, related to or through his father, mother and/or children. Considering parents, native's father/mother may be a rich man/woman, a celebrity, an officer in government or a powerful politician. The native may enjoy many benefits because of his father/mother's money, influence and/or status. He/she may give a big amount of money, and/or wealth to the native, while he/she's alive, and/or through his/her will. Considering children, the native may have children who may be physically, intellectually, emotionally, creatively and/or spiritually better or much better than average. Such children may achieve a lot in many spheres of their lives, and they may bring good name and many other good results to the native.

Looking at profession, such combust Moon can help the native achieve success as a fire fighter, fitness trainer, body builder, sportsman, athlete, physician, dietician, lawyer, astrologer, tantric, psychic, spiritual guru, healer, religious guru, teacher, preacher, consultant, researcher, analyst, host, artist, poet, chef, interior designer, professional dealing in education industry, coaching, food, health, pharma, medical, nursing, homecare, real estate, agriculture, hospitality, beauty, fashion, finance, television, music, sports, media, book, publishing, fitness, travel, hotel, airline, fishing, shipping, telecom, computer, software, IT, internet industry or some other type of professional, depending on his/her overall horoscope and running times.

Such combust Moon can help the native achieve success through a creative field as an actor, singer, musician, writer, dancer, sportsman, artist, architect, designer, developer or some other likewise professional. Taking an example, suppose benefic combust Moon is placed in the sixth house of a horoscope in Leo with Sun. Benefic Mercury is placed in the fifth house in Cancer with Venus; benefic retrograde Jupiter is placed in the seventh house in Virgo with benefic Mars; benefic Rahu is placed in the second house in Aries, Ketu is placed in the eighth house in Libra, and Saturn is placed in the fourth house in Gemini.

In this case, the native may become an actor. He may possess remarkable acting talent, and he may come across very good amount of success, money, recognition and fame. He may perform very well in the genres of action, romance, comedy and drama. He may deliver several hit movies, and he may receive many awards. If the finer factors and running times are supportive, he may become one of the most successful actors of his time, and his net worth may be in multimillions.

Such combust Moon can bless the native with authority in government as a police officer, army, air force, naval, revenue, administrative, foreign services officer, judge, doctor, scientist, engineer, politician or some other type of professional. Taking an example, suppose benefic combust Moon is placed in the sixth house of a horoscope in Leo with Sun and benefic retrograde Mercury. Benefic Mars is placed in the first house in Pisces with benefic Jupiter; retrograde Venus is placed in the seventh house in Virgo, benefic Rahu is placed in the eighth house in Libra, Ketu is placed in the second house in Aries, and Saturn is placed in the twelfth house in Aquarius.

In this case, the native may achieve success in competitive exams, and he may get selected for the highest possible direct rank in naval force. He may serve at several important posts during his career, and he may come across very good amount of success, recognition and authority. If the finer factors and running times are supportive, he may serve as the chief of naval force of his country, before retirement.

On the other hand, when malefic in nature, combination of Sun and combust Moon in the sixth house of a horoscope in Leo can trouble the native with problems related to father, mother, love life, children, profession, finances, reputation, authority, recognition and several other problems, depending on his/her overall horoscope and running times.

Sun rules the sixth house, Moon rules the fifth house, and they are placed in the sixth house. If such combination of Sun and combust Moon is influenced by malefic planets, and/or an overall malefic horoscope, the native may witness various types of problems related to or through his father, mother and/or children. Considering parents, the native may not have a good equation with his father/mother, his parents may get divorced and he may live with his father/mother, his father/mother may suffer from a long-lasting illness, he/she may be an alcoholic and/or a drug addict, he/she may be a criminal, and/or he/she may die before native's age of 20, depending on native's overall horoscope and running times. The native may not know his biological father/mother, or his father/mother may refuse to accept him as his/her son, as native may be born from a secret love affair of his father/mother, and he/she may give him to someone else or to an orphanage. Considering children, the native may lose one or more children through miscarriages that his wife may witness. He may witness delay in childbirth, and/or he may have children who may be physically and/or mentally troubled in some way. He may lose his children through divorce, or his children may engage in immoral/illegal activities, and he may witness bad reputation and many other problems because of them. In an extreme case, the native may witness death of one or more children during their young ages.

The native may witness delays, financial losses, setbacks, failures, job loss, bad reputation and several other problems related to or through his profession. Taking an example, suppose combust Moon is placed in the sixth house of a horoscope in Leo with Mercury, malefic Sun and malefic Venus. Malefic exalted Ketu is placed in the first house in Pisces, malefic exalted Rahu is placed in the seventh house in Virgo with Mars; Jupiter is placed in the eighth house in Libra, and malefic retrograde Saturn is placed in the fourth house in Gemini. Angarak Yoga is formed in the seventh house.

In this case, native's mother may die before his age of 10 or 5, and his father may die before native's age of 20 or 15. The native may not find a permanent profession till his age of 35/40, or throughout his life, and he may keep losing jobs. He may remain jobless for periods of more than 3 months, many times in his life, though he may earn well at times. He may witness 1 or 2 failed marriages. He may lose one or more children to death, through miscarriages that his wife/wives may witness.

Combust Moon in Sixth House in Virgo

When Sun and combust Moon are placed in the sixth house of a horoscope in Virgo, Aries rises in the ascendant. Sun rules the fifth house, and Moon rules the fourth house. In general, this combination is benefic here, in many cases. The concept of various planets exhibiting tendencies to be benefic or malefic on the basis of the houses they rule in a horoscope has been explained in the book 'Gemstones: Magic or Science?'.

Combination of Sun and combust Moon in the sixth house of horoscope in Virgo is benefic in many cases, though it may turn malefic in some cases. It may happen when such combination is influenced by one or more malefic planets, and/or an overall malefic horoscope. The concept of a benefic planet turning malefic due to influences of malefic planets has been explained in the book 'Match Making and Manglik Dosh'.

When benefic in nature, combination of Sun and combust Moon in the sixth house of a horoscope in Virgo can bless the native with good results related to father, mother, education, wealth, properties, vehicles, love life, children, creativity, profession, finances, reputation, authority, recognition, fame and several other good results, depending on his/her overall horoscope and running times.

Such combination of Sun and combust Moon can render various types of benefits to the native, related to or through his father, mother and/or children. Considering parents, native's father/mother may be a rich man/woman, a celebrity, an officer in government or a powerful politician. The native may enjoy many benefits because of his father/mother's money, influence and/or status. He/she may give a big amount of money, and/or wealth to the native, while he/she's alive, and/or through his/her will. Such combination of Sun and combust Moon can bless the native with good education, vehicles, residential house/houses and/or several other good results. Considering children, the native may have children who may be physically, intellectually, emotionally, creatively and/or spiritually better or much better than average. Such children may achieve a lot in many spheres of their lives, and they may bring good name and many other good results to the native.

Looking at profession, such combust Moon can help the native achieve success as a fire fighter, fitness trainer, body builder, sportsman, athlete, physician, dietician, lawyer, astrologer, tantric, psychic, spiritual guru, healer, religious guru, teacher, preacher, consultant, actor, singer, musician, writer, dancer, sportsman, artist, architect, designer, developer, poet, chef, interior designer, host, researcher, analyst, professional dealing in education industry, coaching, food, health, pharma, medical, nursing, homecare, real estate, agriculture, hospitality, beauty, fashion, finance, television, music, sports, media, book, publishing, fitness, travel, hotel, airline, fishing, shipping, telecom, computer, software, IT, internet industry or some other type of professional, depending on his/her overall horoscope and running times.

Taking an example, suppose benefic combust Moon is placed in the sixth house of a horoscope in Virgo with benefic Sun and benefic debilitated Venus. Benefic exalted Rahu is placed in the second house in Taurus, exalted Ketu is placed in the eighth house in Scorpio, Mars is placed in the fifth house in Leo, and Jupiter is placed in the seventh house in Libra with Mercury. In this case, the native may start a restaurant dealing in fast food and bakery items. He may witness good results.

If benefic retrograde Saturn forms Shasha Yoga in the tenth house in Capricorn, the equation may become better. In this case, the native may come across very good amount of success, money and recognition. His business may expand after his age of 35/40, and it may keep growing. If the finer factors and running times are supportive, he may own a chain of restaurants, worth in billions, by his age of 55/60.

Such combust Moon can bless the native with authority in government as a police officer, army, air force, naval, revenue, administrative, foreign services officer, judge, doctor, scientist, engineer, politician or some other type of professional. Taking an example, suppose benefic combust Moon is placed in the sixth house of a horoscope in Virgo with benefic Sun. Benefic Venus is placed in the seventh house in Libra with retrograde Mercury; benefic Saturn is placed in the second house in Taurus with Mars and debilitated Ketu; benefic debilitated Rahu is placed in the eighth house in Scorpio, and Jupiter is placed in the eleventh house in Aquarius. Venus forms Malavya Yoga in the seventh house.

In this case, the native may achieve success in civil exams, and he may get selected for the highest possible direct rank in revenue services. He may serve at several important posts during his career, and he may come across very good amount of success, recognition and authority. If the finer factors and running times are supportive, he may serve as the head of a revenue department, before retirement.

On the other hand, when malefic in nature, combination of Sun and combust Moon in the sixth house of a horoscope in Virgo can trouble the native with problems related to father, mother, education, wealth, properties, vehicles, love life, children, profession, finances, reputation, authority, recognition and several other problems, depending on his/her overall horoscope and running times.

Sun rules the fifth house, Moon rules the fourth house, and they are placed in the sixth house. If such combination of Sun and combust Moon is influenced by malefic planets, and/or an overall malefic horoscope, the native may witness various types of problems related to or through his father, mother and/or children. Considering parents, the native may not have a good equation with his father/mother, his parents may get divorced and he may live with his father/mother, his father/mother may suffer from a long-lasting illness, he/she may be an alcoholic and/or a drug addict, he/she may be a criminal, and/or he/she may die before native's age of 20, depending on native's overall horoscope and running times. Considering children, the native may lose one or more children through miscarriages that his wife may witness. He may witness delay in childbirth, and/or he may have children who may be physically and/or mentally troubled in some way. He may lose his children through divorce, or his children may engage in immoral/illegal activities, and he may witness bad reputation and many other problems because of them. In an extreme case, the native may witness death of one or more children during their young ages.

The native may witness delays, financial losses, setbacks, failures, job loss, bad reputation and several other problems related to or through his profession. Taking an example, suppose combust Moon is placed in the sixth house of a horoscope in Virgo with Sun, malefic retrograde Mercury and malefic exalted Rahu. Malefic exalted Ketu is placed in the twelfth house in Pisces with Saturn; Venus is placed in the eighth house in Scorpio, exalted Jupiter is placed in the fourth house in Cancer, and Mars is placed in the seventh house in Libra. Grahan Yoga is formed in the sixth house.

In this case, native's mother may die before his age of 15/10. His father may get married again, but the native may not have a good equation with his stepmother. He may not find a permanent profession throughout his life, and he may only find temporary jobs. He may remain jobless for periods of more than 6 months, many times in his life. He may witness 1 or 2 failed marriages. He may lose one or more children to death, through miscarriages that his wife/ wives may witness.

Combust Moon in Sixth House in Libra

When Sun and combust Moon are placed in the sixth house of a horoscope in Libra, Taurus rises in the ascendant. Sun rules the fourth house, and Moon rules the third house. In general, this combination is benefic here, in many cases. The concept of various planets exhibiting tendencies to be benefic or malefic on the basis of the houses they rule in a horoscope has been explained in the book 'Gemstones: Magic or Science?'.

Combination of Sun and combust Moon in the sixth house of horoscope in Libra is benefic in many cases, though it may turn malefic in some cases. It may happen when such combination is influenced by one or more malefic planets, and/or an overall malefic horoscope. The concept of a benefic planet turning malefic due to influences of malefic planets has been explained in the book 'Match Making and Manglik Dosh'.

When benefic in nature, combination of Sun and combust Moon in the sixth house of a horoscope in Libra can bless the native with good results related to father, mother, education, wealth, properties, vehicles, siblings, colleagues, profession, finances, reputation, authority, recognition, fame and several other good results, depending on his/her overall horoscope and running times.

Such combination of Sun and combust Moon can render various types of benefits to the native, related to or through his father, mother and/or siblings. Considering parents, native's father/mother may be a rich man/woman, a celebrity, an officer in government or a powerful politician. The native may enjoy many benefits because of his father/mother's money, influence and/or status. He/she may give a big amount of money, and/or wealth to the native, while he/she's alive, and/or through his/her will. This combination can bless the native with good education, vehicles, residential house/houses and/or several other good results. Considering siblings, some of them may stand by the native and they may help him get out of his problems, many times in his life. A sibling of the native may give him a big amount of money, and/or wealth, while such sibling is alive, and/or through his/her will.

Looking at profession, such combust Moon can help the native achieve success as a fire fighter, fitness trainer, body builder, sportsman, athlete, physician, dietician, lawyer, astrologer, tantric, psychic, spiritual guru, healer, religious guru, teacher, preacher, consultant, actor, singer, musician, writer, dancer, sportsman, artist, architect, designer, developer, poet, chef, interior designer, host, researcher, analyst, professional dealing in education industry, coaching, food, health, pharma, medical, nursing, homecare, real estate, agriculture, hospitality, beauty, fashion, finance, television, music, sports, media, book, publishing, fitness, travel, hotel, airline, fishing, shipping, telecom, computer, software,

IT, internet industry or some other type of professional, depending on his/her overall horoscope and running times.

Taking an example, suppose benefic combust Moon is placed in the seventh house of a horoscope in Libra with Venus and benefic debilitated Sun. Benefic exalted Mercury is placed in the fifth house in Virgo with debilitated Ketu; benefic debilitated Rahu is placed in the eleventh house in Pisces, benefic Saturn is placed in the second house in Gemini with retrograde Jupiter, and Mars is placed in the eighth house in Sagittarius.

In this case, the native may start a company which may manufacture various types of liquor products, and he may come across very good amount of success, money and recognition. His business may expand after his age of 35/40, and it may keep growing. If the finer factors and running times are supportive, he may own a business empire worth in billions, by his age of 55/60.

Such combust Moon can bless the native with authority in government as a police officer, army, air force, naval, revenue, administrative, foreign services officer, judge, doctor, scientist, engineer, politician or some other type of professional. Taking an example, suppose benefic combust Moon is placed in the sixth house of a horoscope in Libra with benefic Sun and benefic Mercury. Benefic Saturn is placed in the seventh house in Scorpio with Venus; benefic Rahu is placed in the tenth house in Aquarius, Ketu is placed in the fourth house in Leo with Mars; and retrograde Jupiter is placed in the ninth house in Capricorn. Sun and Mercury form Budhaditya Yoga in the sixth house.

In this case, the native may engage in politics, and he may come across very good amount of success, recognition, authority and fame. He may win several elections, and he may become a minister in national government. He may hold ministry of law, health, home or defence affairs. If the finer factors and running times are supportive, he may become minister, more than once.

On the other hand, when malefic in nature, combination of Sun and combust Moon in the sixth house of a horoscope in Libra can trouble the native with problems related to father, mother, education, wealth, properties, vehicles, siblings, colleagues, profession, finances, reputation, authority, recognition and several other problems, depending on his/her overall horoscope and running times.

Sun rules the fourth house, Moon rules the third house, and they are placed in the sixth house. If such combination of Sun and combust Moon is influenced by malefic planets, and/or an overall malefic horoscope, the native may witness various types of problems related to or through his father, mother and/or siblings. Considering parents, the native may not have a good equation with his father/mother, his parents may get divorced and he may live with his father/mother, his father/mother may suffer from a long-lasting illness, he/she may be an alcoholic and/or a drug addict, he/she may be a criminal, and/or he/she may die before native's age of 20, depending on native's overall horoscope and running times. The native may not know his biological father/mother, or his father/mother may refuse to accept him as his/her son, as native may be born from a secret love affair of his father/mother, and he/she may give him to someone else or to an orphanage. Considering siblings, the native may have bad relationships with some of his siblings, and/or he may witness various types of problems through them or due to them. The native may have siblings who may be criminals, and/or drug addicts, and he may face several problems because of them. In an extreme case, the native may lose one or more siblings to death, before his age of 40 or 35.

The native may witness delays, financial losses, setbacks, failures, job loss, bad reputation and several other problems related to or through his profession. Taking an example, suppose combust Moon is placed in the sixth house of a horoscope in Libra with debilitated Sun, malefic Jupiter and malefic Mars. Venus is placed in the seventh house in Scorpio with benefic Mercury; malefic Rahu is placed in the eighth house in Sagittarius, malefic Ketu is placed in the second house in Gemini, and debilitated Saturn is placed in the twelfth house in Aries.

In this case, native's father as well as mother may die before his age of 20 or 15. The native may not find a permanent profession throughout his life, and he may only find temporary jobs, though he may earn well at times. He may remain jobless for periods of more than 3 months, many times in his life. He may lose one or more siblings to death, before his age of 35/30. He may witness 1 or 2 failed marriages.

Combust Moon in Sixth House in Scorpio

When Sun and combust Moon are placed in the sixth house of a horoscope in Scorpio, Gemini rises in the ascendant. Sun rules the third house, and Moon rules the second house. In general, this combination is benefic here, in many cases. The concept of various planets exhibiting tendencies to be benefic or malefic on the basis of the houses they rule in a horoscope has been explained in the book 'Gemstones: Magic or Science?'.

Combination of Sun and combust Moon in the sixth house of horoscope in Scorpio is benefic in many cases, though it may turn malefic in some cases. It may happen when such combination is influenced by one or more malefic planets, and/or an overall malefic horoscope. The concept of a benefic planet turning malefic due to influences of malefic planets has been explained in the book 'Match Making and Manglik Dosh'.

When benefic in nature, combination of Sun and combust Moon in the sixth house of a horoscope in Scorpio can bless the native with good results related to father, mother, family, wealth, speech, siblings, colleagues, profession, finances, reputation, authority, recognition, fame and several other good results, depending on his/her overall horoscope and running times.

Such combination of Sun and combust Moon can render various types of benefits to the native, related to or through his father, mother, siblings and/or family. Considering parents, native's father/mother may be a rich man/woman, a celebrity, an officer in government or a powerful politician. The native may enjoy many benefits because of his father/mother's money, influence and/or status. He/she may give a big amount of money, and/or wealth to the native, while he/she's alive, and/or through his/her will. Considering siblings, some of them may stand by the native and they may help him get out of his problems, many times in his life. A sibling of the native may give him a big amount of money, and/or wealth, while such sibling is alive, and/or through his/her will.

Looking at profession, such combust Moon can help the native achieve success as a fire fighter, fitness trainer, body builder, sportsman, athlete, physician, dietician, lawyer, astrologer, tantric, psychic, spiritual guru, healer, religious guru, teacher, preacher, consultant, researcher, analyst, host, artist, poet, chef, interior designer, professional dealing in education industry, coaching, food, health, pharma, medical, nursing, homecare, real estate, agriculture, hospitality, beauty, fashion, finance, television, music, sports, media, book, publishing, fitness, travel, hotel, airline, fishing, shipping, telecom, computer, software, IT, internet industry or some other type of professional, depending on his/her overall horoscope and running times.

Such combust Moon can help the native achieve success through a creative field as an actor, singer, musician, writer,

dancer, sportsman, artist, architect, designer, developer or some other likewise professional. Taking an example for a female native, suppose benefic combust Moon is placed in the sixth house of a horoscope in Scorpio with Venus, benefic Sun and benefic Mercury. Benefic Jupiter is placed in the fifth house in Libra, benefic Rahu is placed in the eighth house in Capricorn, Ketu is placed in the second house in Cancer, Saturn is placed in the fourth house in Virgo, and Mars is placed in the ninth house in Aquarius. Budhaditya Yoga is formed in the sixth house.

In this case, the native may write fictional books. She may possess remarkable talent, and she may come across very good amount of success, money, recognition and fame. She may write in several genres, including mystery, suspense and thriller. She may deliver several bestsellers, and she may receive many awards. If the finer factors and running times are supportive, she may become one of the most successful writers of her time, and her net worth may be in multimillions.

Such combust Moon can bless the native with authority in government as a police officer, army, air force, naval, revenue, administrative, foreign services officer, judge, doctor, scientist, engineer, politician or some other type of professional. Taking an example, suppose benefic combust Moon is placed in the sixth house of a horoscope in Scorpio with benefic Sun. Benefic Mercury is placed in the seventh house in Sagittarius with retrograde Venus; benefic Jupiter is placed in the first house in Gemini, retrograde Saturn is placed in the fourth house in Virgo with Mars; benefic Rahu is placed in the ninth house in Aquarius, and Ketu is placed in the third house in Leo.

In this case, the native may achieve success in civil exams, and he may get selected for the highest possible direct rank in foreign services. He may serve at several important posts during his career, and he may come across very good amount of success, recognition and authority. He may represent his country in several countries of the world. If the finer factors and running times are supportive, he may serve at one of the top 2 ranks in foreign services, before retirement.

On the other hand, when malefic in nature, combination of Sun and combust Moon in the sixth house of a horoscope in Scorpio can trouble the native with problems related to father, mother, family, wealth, speech, siblings, colleagues, profession, finances, reputation, authority, recognition and several other problems, depending on his/her overall horoscope and running times.

Sun rules the third house, Moon rules the second house, and they are placed in the sixth house. If such combination of Sun and combust Moon is influenced by malefic planets, and/or an overall malefic horoscope, the native may witness various types of problems related to or through his father, mother, siblings and/or family. Considering parents, the native may not have a good equation with his father/mother, his parents may get divorced and he may live with his father/mother, his father/mother may suffer from a long-lasting illness, he/she may be an alcoholic and/or a drug addict, he/she may be a criminal, and/or he/she may die before native's age of 20, depending on native's overall horoscope and running times. The native may not know his biological father/mother, or his father/mother may refuse to accept him as his/her son, as native may be born from a secret love affair of his father/mother, and he/she may give him to someone else or to an orphanage. Considering siblings, the native may have bad relationships with some of his siblings, and/or he may witness various types of problems through them or due to them. The native may have siblings who may be criminals, and/or drug addicts, and he may face several problems because of them. In an extreme case, the native may lose one or more siblings to death, before his age of 40 or 35.

The native may witness delays, financial losses, setbacks, failures, job loss, bad reputation and several other problems related to or through his profession. Taking an example, suppose combust Moon is placed in the sixth house of a horoscope in Scorpio with Sun, malefic Mars and malefic debilitated Rahu. Malefic debilitated Ketu is placed in the twelfth house in Taurus with retrograde Saturn; Venus is placed in the seventh house in Sagittarius with benefic Mercury; and benefic Jupiter is placed in the fifth house in Libra. Grahan Yoga is formed in the sixth house.

In this case, native's father as well as mother may die before his age of 20/15. He may not achieve much professional success till his age of 35/40, or throughout his life, though he may earn well at times. He may witness financial losses and setbacks through profession. He may lose one or more siblings to death, before his age of 35/30. He may witness 1 or 2 failed marriages.

Combust Moon in Sixth House in Sagittarius

When Sun and combust Moon are placed in the sixth house of a horoscope in Sagittarius, Cancer rises in the ascendant. Sun rules the second house, and Moon rules the first house. In general, this combination is benefic here, in many cases. The concept of various planets exhibiting tendencies to be benefic or malefic on the basis of the houses they rule in a horoscope has been explained in the book 'Gemstones: Magic or Science?'.

Combination of Sun and combust Moon in the sixth house of horoscope in Sagittarius is benefic in many cases, though it may turn malefic in some cases. It may happen when such combination is influenced by one or more malefic planets, and/or an overall malefic horoscope. The concept of a benefic planet turning malefic due to influences of malefic planets has been explained in the book 'Match Making and Manglik Dosh'.

When benefic in nature, combination of Sun and combust Moon in the sixth house of a horoscope in Sagittarius can bless the native with good results related to father, mother, health, lifespan, family, wealth, speech, profession, finances, reputation, authority, recognition, fame and several other good results, depending on his/her overall horoscope and running times.

Such combination of Sun and combust Moon can render various types of benefits to the native, related to or through his father, mother, family and/or lifespan. Considering parents, native's father/mother may be a rich man/woman, a celebrity, an officer in government or a powerful politician. The native may enjoy many benefits because of his father/mother's money, influence and/or status. He/she may give a big amount of money, and/or wealth to the native, while he/she's alive, and/or through his/her will. Considering family, the native may be born in a rich, influential, resourceful, well-respected, politically powerful, royal and/or spiritually advanced family, and he may witness several benefits by virtue of being a member of such family.

Looking at profession, such combust Moon can help the native achieve success as a fire fighter, fitness trainer, body builder, sportsman, athlete, physician, dietician, lawyer, astrologer, tantric, psychic, spiritual guru, healer, religious guru, teacher, preacher, consultant, researcher, analyst, host, artist, poet, chef, interior designer, professional dealing in education industry, coaching, food, health, pharma, medical, nursing, homecare, real estate, agriculture, hospitality, beauty, fashion, finance, television, music, sports, media, book, publishing, fitness, travel, hotel, airline, fishing, shipping, telecom, computer, software, IT, internet industry or some other type of professional, depending on his/her overall horoscope and running times.

Such combust Moon can help the native achieve success through a creative field as an actor, singer, musician, writer,

dancer, sportsman, artist, architect, designer, developer or some other likewise professional. Taking an example, suppose benefic combust Moon is placed in the sixth house of a horoscope in Sagittarius with benefic Sun. Benefic Venus is placed in the fifth house in Scorpio with Mercury and benefic debilitated Rahu; benefic Mars is placed in the eleventh house in Taurus with debilitated Ketu; Jupiter is placed in the fourth house in Libra, and Saturn is placed in the eighth house in Aquarius.

In this case, the native may become a singer. He may possess remarkable talent, and he may come across very good amount of success, money, recognition and fame. He may deliver several hit songs, and he may receive many awards. If the finer factors and running times are supportive, he may become one of the most successful singers of his time, and his net worth may be in multimillions.

Such combust Moon can bless the native with authority in government as a police officer, army, air force, naval, revenue, administrative, foreign services officer, judge, doctor, scientist, engineer, politician or some other type of professional. Taking an example, suppose benefic combust Moon is placed in the sixth house of a horoscope in Sagittarius with Jupiter and benefic Sun. Mercury is placed in the seventh house in Capricorn, benefic debilitated Mars is placed in the first house in Cancer, benefic Venus is placed in the fourth house in Libra with Ketu; benefic Rahu is placed in the tenth house in Aries, and Saturn is placed in the second house in Leo. Venus forms Malavya Yoga in the fourth house.

In this case, the native may achieve success in civil exams, and he may get selected for the highest possible direct rank in revenue services. He may serve at several important posts during his career, and he may come across very good amount of success, recognition and authority. If the finer factors and running times are supportive, he may serve at one of the top 2 ranks in revenue services, before retirement.

On the other hand, when malefic in nature, combination of Sun and combust Moon in the sixth house of a horoscope in Sagittarius can trouble the native with problems related to father, mother, health, lifespan, family, wealth, speech, profession, finances, reputation, authority, recognition and several other problems, depending on his/her overall horoscope and running times.

Sun rules the second house, Moon rules the first house, and they are placed in the sixth house. If such combination of Sun and combust Moon is influenced by malefic planets, and/or an overall malefic horoscope, the native may witness various types of problems related to or through his father, mother, family and/or lifespan. Considering parents, the native may not have a good equation with his father/mother, his parents may get divorced and he may live with his father/mother, his father/mother may suffer from a long-lasting illness, he/she may be an alcoholic and/or a drug addict, he/she may be a criminal, and/or he/she may die before native's age of 20, depending on native's overall horoscope and running times.The native may not know his biological father/mother, or his father/mother may refuse to accept him as his/her son, as native may be born from a secret love affair of his father/mother, and he/she may give him to someone else or to an orphanage. Considering lifespan, the native may witness reduction in lifespan due to several reasons. For example, the native may die in an accident, through a natural disaster, due to a fatal disease, due to a fatal viral infection like COVID, due to drug addiction, he may commit suicide, or someone may kill him intentionally or unintentionally. Considering some unintentional incidents, he may get caught in a crossfire between two rival criminal gangs or that between criminals and police, or someone may accidently kill him.

The native may witness delays, financial losses, setbacks, failures, job loss, bad reputation and several other problems related to or through his profession. Taking an example, suppose combust Moon is placed in the sixth house of a horoscope in Sagittarius with Sun, malefic Mercury and malefic retrograde Saturn. Malefic Rahu is placed in the seventh house in Capricorn with Venus; malefic Ketu is placed in the first house in Cancer, Jupiter is placed in the fourth house in Libra, and Mars is placed in the eighth house in Aquarius.

In this case, native's mother may die before his age of 15/10. His father may get married again, but the native may not have a good equation with his stepmother. He may not find a permanent profession till his age of 35/40, or throughout his life, though he may earn well at times. He may remain jobless for periods of more than 3 months, many times in his life. He may witness 2 or 3 failed marriages. He may die before his age of 55 or 50, due to a heart attack, some type of cancer, another fatal disease, in an accident, or because of a fatal viral infection like COVID.

Combust Moon in Sixth House in Capricorn

When Sun and combust Moon are placed in the sixth house of a horoscope in Capricorn, Leo rises in the ascendant. Sun rules the first house, and Moon rules the twelfth house. In general, this combination is partly benefic and partly malefic here, though the malefic part is higher, in most cases. The concept of various planets exhibiting tendencies to be benefic or malefic on the basis of the houses they rule in a horoscope has been explained in the book 'Gemstones: Magic or Science?'.

Combination of Sun and combust Moon in the sixth house of horoscope in Capricorn is malefic in many cases, though it may turn benefic in some cases. It may happen when such combination is influenced by one or more benefic planets, and/or an overall benefic horoscope. The concept of a malefic planet turning benefic due to influences of benefic planets has been explained in the book 'Match Making and Manglik Dosh'.

When benefic in nature, combination of Sun and combust Moon in the sixth house of a horoscope in Capricorn can bless the native with good results related to father, mother, health, lifespan, profession, finances, reputation, authority, recognition, fame and several other good results, depending on his/her overall horoscope and running times.

Such combination of Sun and combust Moon can render various types of benefits to the native, related to or through his father, mother and/or lifespan. Considering parents, native's father/mother may be a rich man/woman, a celebrity, an officer in government or a powerful politician. The native may enjoy many benefits because of his father/mother's money, influence and/or status. He/she may give a big amount of money, and/or wealth to the native, while he/she's alive, and/or through his/her will.

Looking at profession, such combust Moon can help the native achieve success as a fire fighter, fitness trainer, body builder, sportsman, athlete, physician, dietician, lawyer, astrologer, tantric, psychic, spiritual guru, healer, religious guru, teacher, preacher, consultant, actor, singer, musician, writer, dancer, sportsman, artist, architect, designer, developer, poet, chef, interior designer, host, researcher, analyst, professional dealing in education industry, coaching, food, health, pharma, medical, nursing, homecare, real estate, agriculture, hospitality, beauty, fashion, finance, television, music, sports, media, book, publishing, fitness, travel, hotel, airline, fishing, shipping, telecom, computer, software, IT, internet industry or some other type of professional, depending on his/her overall horoscope and running times.

Taking an example, suppose combust Moon is placed in the sixth house of a horoscope in Capricorn with benefic Sun. Benefic Mercury is placed in the fifth house in Sagittarius, benefic Venus is placed in the seventh house in Aquarius, benefic Mars is placed in the ninth house in Aries, benefic debilitated Rahu is placed in the eighth house in Pisces, debilitated Ketu is placed in the second house in Virgo, retrograde Saturn is placed in the first house in Leo, and retrograde Jupiter is placed in the twelfth house in Cancer.

In this case, the native may become a scientist. He may specialize in botany, he may possess remarkable knowledge of his field, and he may come across very good amount of success and recognition, along with good amount of money. He may conduct research, and he may come across discoveries. If the finer factors and running times are supportive, he may serve as the head of his department for several years.

Such combust Moon can bless the native with authority in government as a police officer, army, air force, naval, revenue, administrative, foreign services officer, judge, doctor, scientist, engineer, politician or some other type of professional. Taking an example, suppose combust Moon is placed in the sixth house of a horoscope in Capricorn with benefic Sun and benefic Venus. Benefic retrograde Mercury is placed in the fifth house in Sagittarius with Saturn; benefic Mars is placed in the first house in Leo with benefic Rahu, Ketu is placed in the seventh house in Aquarius, and Jupiter is placed in the ninth house in Aries.

In this case, the native may achieve success in competitive exams, and he may get selected for the highest possible direct rank in air force. He may be a skilled fighter pilot, and he may succeed in several missions. He may serve at several important posts during his career, and he may come across very good amount of success, recognition and authority. If the finer factors and running times are supportive, he may serve at one of the top 2 ranks in air force, before retirement.

On the other hand, when malefic in nature, combination of Sun and combust Moon in the sixth house of a horoscope in Capricorn can trouble the native with problems related to father, mother, health, lifespan, profession, finances, reputation, authority, recognition and several other problems, depending on his/her overall horoscope and running times.

Sun rules the first house, Moon rules the twelfth house, and they are placed in the sixth house. If such combination of Sun and combust Moon is influenced by malefic planets, and/or an overall malefic horoscope, the native may witness various types of problems related to or through his father, mother and/or lifespan. Considering parents, the native may not have a good equation with his father/mother, his parents may get divorced and he may live with his father/mother, his father/mother may suffer from a long-lasting illness, he/she may be an alcoholic and/or a drug addict, he/she may be a criminal, and/or he/she may die before native's age of 20, depending on native's overall horoscope and running times. The native may not know his biological father/mother, or his father/mother may refuse to accept him as his/her son, as native may be born from a secret love affair of his father/mother, and he/she may give him to someone else or to an orphanage. In an extreme case, the native may kill his father/mother for some reason, or his father/mother may kill him, depending on native's overall horoscope and running times. Considering lifespan, the native may witness reduction in lifespan due to several reasons. For example, the native may die in an accident, through a natural disaster, due to a fatal disease, due to a fatal viral infection like COVID, due to drug addiction, he may commit suicide, or someone may kill him intentionally or unintentionally. Considering some unintentional incidents, he may get caught in a crossfire between two rival criminal gangs or that between criminals and police, or someone may accidently kill him.

The native may witness delays, financial losses, setbacks, failures, job loss, bad reputation and several other problems related to or through his profession. Taking an example, suppose malefic combust Moon is placed in the sixth house of a horoscope in Capricorn with Sun, retrograde Venus and debilitated Jupiter. Malefic Saturn is placed in the seventh house in Aquarius with Mercury; malefic debilitated Rahu is placed in the fourth house in Scorpio, malefic debilitated Ketu is placed in the tenth house in Taurus, and Mars is placed in the eighth house in Pisces.

In this case, native's father may die before native's age of 10 or 5. His mother may get married again, but the native may not have a good equation with his stepfather. Native's mother may die before his age of 25/20. He may not find a permanent profession till his age of 35/40, or throughout his life. He may remain jobless for periods of more than 6 months, many times in his life. He may not get married till his age of 35/40, or throughout his life. He may die before his age of 55 or 50, due to a heart attack, some type of cancer, or because of a fatal viral infection like COVID.

Combust Moon in Sixth House in Aquarius

When Sun and combust Moon are placed in the sixth house of a horoscope in Aquarius, Virgo rises in the ascendant. Sun rules the twelfth house, and Moon rules the eleventh house. In general, this combination is partly benefic and partly malefic here, though the malefic part is higher, in most cases. The concept of various planets exhibiting tendencies to be benefic or malefic on the basis of the houses they rule in a horoscope has been explained in the book 'Gemstones: Magic or Science?'.

Combination of Sun and combust Moon in the sixth house of horoscope in Aquarius is malefic in many cases, though it may turn benefic in some cases. It may happen when such combination is influenced by one or more benefic planets, and/or an overall benefic horoscope. The concept of a malefic planet turning benefic due to influences of benefic planets has been explained in the book 'Match Making and Manglik Dosh'.

When benefic in nature, combination of Sun and combust Moon in the sixth house of a horoscope in Aquarius can bless the native with good results related to father, mother, friends, profession, finances, reputation, authority, recognition, fame and several other good results, depending on his/her overall horoscope and running times.

Such combination of Sun and combust Moon can render various types of benefits to the native, related to or through his father, mother and/or friends. Considering parents, native's father/mother may be a rich man/woman, a celebrity, an officer in government or a powerful politician. The native may enjoy many benefits because of his father/mother's money, influence and/or status. He/she may give a big amount of money, and/or wealth to the native, while he/she's alive, and/or through his/her will. Considering friends, some of his friends may stand by the native and they may help him get out of his problems, many times in his life. One or more of his friends may help him financially as well as in other ways, in order for him to start a new business, or repair/consolidate an already existing business.

Looking at profession, such combust Moon can help the native achieve success as a fire fighter, fitness trainer, body builder, sportsman, athlete, physician, dietician, lawyer, astrologer, tantric, psychic, spiritual guru, healer, religious guru, teacher, preacher, consultant, researcher, analyst, host, artist, poet, chef, interior designer, professional dealing in education industry, coaching, food, health, pharma, medical, nursing, homecare, real estate, agriculture, hospitality, beauty, fashion, finance, television, music, sports, media, book, publishing, fitness, travel, hotel, airline, fishing, shipping, telecom, computer, software, IT, internet industry or some other type of professional, depending on his/her overall horoscope and running times.

Such combust Moon can help the native achieve success through a creative field as an actor, singer, musician, writer, dancer, sportsman, artist, architect, designer, developer or some other likewise professional. Taking an example, suppose benefic combust Moon is placed in the sixth house of a horoscope in Aquarius with Sun and benefic Mercury. Retrograde Saturn is placed in the second house in Libra, benefic Jupiter forms Hamsa Yoga in the fourth house in Sagittarius, benefic Rahu is placed in the eleventh house in Cancer, Venus is placed in the fifth house in Capricorn with Ketu; and Mars is placed in the eighth house in Aries.

In this case, the native may write fictional books. He may possess remarkable writing talent, and he may come across very good amount of success, money, recognition and fame. He may write in several genres, including action, mystery, thriller, crime and suspense. He may deliver several bestsellers, and he may receive many awards. If the finer factors and running times are supportive, he may become one of the most recognized writers of his time, and his net worth may be in multimillions.

Such combust Moon can bless the native with authority in government as a police officer, army, air force, naval, revenue, administrative, foreign services officer, judge, doctor, scientist, engineer, politician or some other type of professional. Taking an example, suppose benefic combust Moon is placed in the sixth house of a horoscope in Aquarius with Sun. Benefic retrograde Mercury is placed in the fifth house in Capricorn with Saturn and benefic Venus; benefic exalted Rahu is placed in the first house in Virgo with Mars; exalted Ketu is placed in the seventh house in Pisces, and benefic Jupiter forms Hamsa Yoga in the fourth house in Sagittarius.

In this case, the native may engage in politics, and he may come across very good amount of success, recognition, authority and fame. He may win several elections, and he may become chief minister or governor of a state. If the finer factors and running times are supportive, he may hold one such post, more than once in his life.

On the other hand, when malefic in nature, combination of Sun and combust Moon in the sixth house of a horoscope in Aquarius can trouble the native with problems related to father, mother, friends, profession, finances, reputation, authority, recognition and several other problems, depending on his/her overall horoscope and running times.

Sun rules the twelfth house, Moon rules the eleventh house, and they are placed in the sixth house. If such combination of Sun and combust Moon is influenced by malefic planets, and/or an overall malefic horoscope, the native may witness various types of problems related to or through his father, mother and/or friends. Considering parents, the native may not have a good equation with his father/mother, his parents may get divorced and he may live with his father/mother, his father/mother may suffer from a long-lasting illness, he/she may be an alcoholic and/or a drug addict, he/she may be a criminal, and/or he/she may die before native's age of 20, depending on native's overall horoscope and running times. The native may not know his biological father/mother, or his father/mother may refuse to accept him as his/her son, as native may be born from a secret love affair of his father/mother, and he/she may give him to someone else or to an orphanage. In an extreme case, the native may kill his father/mother for some reason, or his father/mother may kill him, depending on native's overall horoscope and running times. Considering friends, some of his friends may be selfish, opportunists, criminal-minded, criminals, drug addicts, traitors and/or they may have some other negative traits. The native may witness several problems because of such friends, many times in his life. Some of his friends may be his hidden enemies, and they may keep causing problems for him. In an extreme case, one or more of his good friends may die before native's age of 40 or 35.

The native may witness delays, financial losses, setbacks, failures, job loss, bad reputation and several other problems related to or through his profession. Taking an example, suppose combust Moon is placed in the sixth house of a horoscope in Aquarius with Venus, malefic Sun and malefic Mars. Debilitated Mercury is placed in the seventh house in Pisces, malefic Rahu is placed in the fourth house in Sagittarius, malefic Ketu and Jupiter form Guru Chandal Yoga in the tenth house in Gemini, and Saturn is placed in the ninth house in Taurus.

In this case, native's mother may die before his age of 15 or 10. His father may get married again, but the native may not have a good equation with his stepmother. He may not achieve much professional success till his age of 35/40, or throughout his life, though he may earn well at times. He may remain jobless for periods of more than 3 months, many times in his life. He may lose one or more good friends to death, before his age of 35/30.

Combust Moon in Sixth House in Pisces

When Sun and combust Moon are placed in the sixth house of a horoscope in Pisces, Libra rises in the ascendant. Sun rules the eleventh house, and Moon rules the tenth house. In general, this combination is benefic here, in many cases. The concept of various planets exhibiting tendencies to be benefic or malefic on the basis of the houses they rule in a horoscope has been explained in the book 'Gemstones: Magic or Science?'.

Combination of Sun and combust Moon in the sixth house of horoscope in Pisces is benefic in many cases, though it may turn malefic in some cases. It may happen when such combination is influenced by one or more malefic planets, and/or an overall malefic horoscope. The concept of a benefic planet turning malefic due to influences of malefic planets has been explained in the book 'Match Making and Manglik Dosh'.

When benefic in nature, combination of Sun and combust Moon in the sixth house of a horoscope in Pisces can bless the native with good results related to father, mother, friends, profession, finances, reputation, authority, recognition, fame and several other good results, depending on his/her overall horoscope and running times.

Such combination of Sun and combust Moon can render various types of benefits to the native, related to or through his father, mother and/or friends. Considering parents, native's father/mother may be a rich man/woman, a celebrity, an officer in government or a powerful politician. The native may enjoy many benefits because of his father/mother's money, influence and/or status. He/she may give a big amount of money, and/or wealth to the native, while he/she's alive, and/or through his/her will. Considering friends, some of his friends may stand by the native and they may help him get out of his problems, many times in his life. One or more of his friends may help him financially as well as in other ways, in order for him to start a new business, or repair/consolidate an already existing business.

Looking at profession, such combust Moon can help the native achieve success as a fire fighter, fitness trainer, body builder, sportsman, athlete, physician, dietician, lawyer, astrologer, tantric, psychic, spiritual guru, healer, religious guru, teacher, preacher, consultant, researcher, analyst, host, artist, poet, chef, interior designer, police officer, army, air force, naval, revenue, administrative, foreign services officer, judge, doctor, scientist, engineer, politician, professional dealing in education industry, coaching, food, health, pharma, medical, nursing, homecare, real estate, agriculture, hospitality, beauty, fashion, finance, television, music, sports, media, book, publishing, fitness, travel, hotel, airline, fishing, shipping, telecom, computer, software, IT, internet industry or some other type of professional, depending on his/her overall horoscope and running times.

Taking an example, suppose benefic combust Moon is placed in the sixth house of a horoscope in Pisces with exalted Venus and benefic Sun. Benefic Mars is placed in the eighth house in Taurus with benefic Saturn and benefic exalted Rahu; retrograde Jupiter is placed in the second house in Scorpio with exalted Ketu; and Mercury is placed in the seventh house in Aries.

In this case, the native may start a casino, and he may come across very good amount of success, money and recognition. His business may expand after his age of 35/40, and it may keep growing. He may also start some hotels. If the finer factors and running times are supportive, he may own several hotels and casinos worth in billions, by his age of 55/60.

Such combust Moon can help the native achieve success through a creative field as an actor, singer, musician, writer, dancer, sportsman, artist, architect, designer, developer or some other likewise professional. Taking an example, suppose benefic combust Moon is placed in the sixth house of a horoscope in Pisces with benefic Sun and benefic debilitated Rahu. Debilitated Ketu is placed in the twelfth house in Virgo, Venus is placed in the fifth house in Aquarius with Mercury; benefic retrograde Saturn forms Shasha Yoga in the fourth house in Capricorn, and benefic Mars is placed in the eleventh house in Leo with Jupiter.

In this case, the native may become a movie producer, and he may come across very good amount of success, money, recognition and fame. He may also direct some movies. He may deliver several hit movies, and he may receive many awards. If the finer factors and running times are supportive, he may own a movie production house worth in billions, by his age of 55/60.

On the other hand, when malefic in nature, combination of Sun and combust Moon in the sixth house of a horoscope in Pisces can trouble the native with problems related to father, mother, friends, profession, finances, reputation, authority, recognition and several other problems, depending on his/ her overall horoscope and running times.

Sun rules the eleventh house, Moon rules the tenth house, and they are placed in the sixth house. If such combination of Sun and combust Moon is influenced by malefic planets, and/or an overall malefic horoscope, the native may witness various types of problems related to or through his father, mother and/or friends. Considering parents, the native may not have a good equation with his father/mother, his parents may get divorced and he may live with his father/mother, his father/mother may suffer from a long-lasting illness, he/she may be an alcoholic and/or a drug addict, he/she may be a criminal, and/or he/she may die before native's age of 20, depending on native's overall horoscope and running times. The native may not know his biological father/mother, or his father/mother may refuse to accept him as his/her son, as native may be born from a secret love affair of his father/ mother, and he/she may give him to someone else or to an orphanage. Considering friends, some of his friends may be selfish, opportunists, criminal-minded, criminals, drug addicts, traitors and/or they may have some other negative traits. The native may witness several problems because of such friends, many times in his life. Some of his friends may be his hidden enemies, and they may keep causing problems for him. In an extreme case, one or more of his good friends may die before native's age of 40 or 35.

The native may witness delays, financial losses, setbacks, failures, job loss, bad reputation and several other problems related to or through his profession. Taking an example, suppose combust Moon is placed in the sixth house of a horoscope in Pisces with Sun, retrograde Mercury, retrograde Venus and malefic exalted Ketu. Malefic exalted Rahu is placed in the twelfth house in Virgo with Mars; retrograde Saturn is placed in the eighth house in Taurus, and malefic debilitated Jupiter is placed in the fourth house in Capricorn. Grahan Yoga is formed in the sixth house, and Angarak Yoga is formed in the twelfth house.

In this case, native's mother may die before his age of 10/5, and his father may die before native's age of 20 or 15. The native may not find a permanent profession till his age of 35/40, or throughout his life, though he may earn well at times. He may remain jobless for periods of more than 3 months, many times in his life. He may lose one or more good friends to death, before his age of 40/35. He may not get married till his age of 35/40, or throughout his life.

Contact Details

Websites

www.AstrologerPanditJi.com

Facebook

https://www.facebook.com/HimanshuShangari

Email IDs

himanshu1847-himanshushangari@yahoo.com

himanshu1847-astrologerpanditji@yahoo.com

himanshushangari1847@gmail.com

www.ingramcontent.com/pod-product-compliance
Lightning Source LLC
La Vergne TN
LVHW041211150826
845673LV00001B/359

9798888839102